Don't Try to Follow Jesus in College

A Practical Guide on Actually Following Him

Gabe Barrett

ISBN: 153273042X
ISBN-13: 978-1532730429

DEDICATION

To all those who helped make my college career
an awesome time to look back on.

CONTENTS

Foreword

For we must all appear before the judgment seat of Christ, so that each may be repaid for what he has done in the body, good or bad.

-2 Corinthians 5:10

The thing I love most about college is the freedom. At no other point in life do you have as few responsibilities and as much freedom to do what you want. Twelve hours a week is considered full time. Almost anything is possible. However, the freedom is what gets a lot of people into trouble. Most don't arrive on campus equipped to deal with all the challenges and struggles that college life presents. Some even have a hard time dealing with the successes.

For whatever reason, churches, parents, teachers, and youth groups don't always get the job done when it comes to preparing young people for higher education. In both academics and spirituality, high school seniors are becoming college freshmen and having their worlds turned upside down. Now, this book doesn't deal with the academic side. Too many people much smarter than I am have written books on how to study and get in good with professors. And I'm not as concerned about your grades. What matters is your spirit.

Too many grounded Christians get to college and completely lose track of their faith. They get around all sorts of brand new people with brand new ideas, and by Christmas break they're questioning whether or not God even exists. Now, a lot of people are quick to blame the church, parents, teachers, and youth groups for not equipping teenagers with the tools they need to face the rigors of the world. But I'm not gonna do that. I'm not going to sit here and bash a whole bunch of people I've never met because at the end of the day, the only person that is going to be held accountable for your actions is YOU.

Your pastor can't step in for you. Your mother can't step in for you. Your teacher can't step in for you. And your youth director can't step in for you. When you stand before God, and He opens up the portfolio of your life's work, you are the only one He's going to talk to. Aunt Shirley and cousin Ray-Ray can't say "let him slide Lord, he didn't know." Mrs. Frizzle can't pass God a note that reads "she almost had it Lord, just pass her on through." This is your life and no one else's. So I don't care if your church never catered to your needs. I don't care if your parents never went to church. I don't care if your teachers were all pretentious washouts. I don't care if all your youth group ever did was play ultimate Frisbee and eat spaghetti. Because when it's all said and done, only YOU can take responsibility for your life's work.

No excuses.

***

Now, I could spout off a bunch of statistics about how many people leave the church once they move off to college. I could fill up these pages with numbers that would make me seem more academic. And I'm sure I could go on Wikipedia and find all sorts of "facts" about today's college student. But I'm just not buying it. I don't put any stock in the stats that say college students don't care about God. Over the last five years, I saw greatness. I met people who were pouring out their lives on a daily basis in pursuit of Jesus. I got to know people with passion, with talent, with intelligence; and their main goal in life was to glorify God.

So I'm not gonna give you a bunch of statistics. Because I'm not writing to a statistic. I'm writing to you. (And in a lot of ways, I'm writing to myself.) Unlike most authors of books on college, I'm not here to be your friend. I'm not your friendly neighborhood tour guide through the next X number of pages. I'm just a guy who made a bunch of mistakes and was able to learn from most of them. You can take it or leave it. That's the thing I love about

Jesus. He always gives people the option. You can take on the life He intends, or you can take on the life *you* intend. The next four years can be about progressing His kingdom, or they can be about proclaiming your own. Either way, the decision rests with you.

***

I'm a big fan of this generation. Don't get me wrong, our parents and grandparents did some great things. They had the toughness. They had the grit. They had the work ethic. They had all the tools that would get us to where we stand now. They laid the ground work for our creativity, our passion, and our enthusiasm. It's time to build on their foundation. College is when you find your hammer and buy your nails. For eighteen or so years, you've been borrowing from your parents' tool shed. It's time to get your own.

I'm going to ask you a lot of questions in this book. And to move forward in your faith, you're going to have to be honest with yourself. Don't think for a second that you can bullcrap God. Answering the tough questions about who you are and what you believe are crucial to the next four years. So I want you to wrestle with this book. Test it. Throw it on the floor. Cuss it out if you have to. I'm not writing something to make you feel good about yourself. There are enough books that already do that. I'm not writing something to make you feel comfortable. And I'm not promising "your best life now" or anything, but I know what it means to live for something greater than myself. I don't have *all* the tools. I don't have *all* the answers. But I know that the next four years are pivotal in your walk with Jesus.

Situations are going to come along and drain the life right out of you. New ideas are going to decimate your views of the world. Professors and classmates are going to challenge you in ways you can't imagine. And if you're not prepared to face all that—to stand strong in your faith and trust God—then this generation doesn't stand a chance. We're on the edge of something big. And the question is not *if* it will happen. The question is whether or not you'll be there when it does. Because once again, you have options: you can be content with what the world calls success or you can chase the only thing that truly satisfies. Either way, it's up to you.

All I ask is that you don't just *try* to follow Jesus in college. Either you do it or you don't. Either devote your life to it or walk away from it. Don't pretend. Don't just play the part. Don't just go through the motions. Don't be luke-warm. And don't straddle the fence. Pick a side, and go after it with everything you've got.

1. Treasure

For where your treasure is, there your heart will be also.

-Mark 6:21

When I was growing up, I stayed with my grandparents a lot. Every morning, before taking me to school, my grandfather would walk outside, raise his hands, and thank God for a beautiful day. What always struck me as odd was that a lot of those days weren't particularly beautiful. Some were rainy. Some were cold. Some were downright miserable. Yet, without fail, he would pray to God in appreciation. My grandfather was less concerned with the humidity or wind chill and much more interested in marveling at God. He just wanted to stand in awe of His presence. It was a constant reminder of how much the Creator meant to him.

College is an extraordinary test of what you really think of God, and I'm not talking about your theology. The next four or so years are going to be full of opportunities to show how much God is worth to you. Because that's really what it all boils down to. You'll have to decide if sin is more important to you than God, if you value money more than God, and if you desire comfort over God. And make no mistake, many Christians decide God just isn't worth it to them. They think a different treasure is more satisfying. What will you choose?

Marvel

We often get so wrapped up in everyday life that we rarely just stop to marvel at God. Especially with all the tests, homework, intramurals, and campus events, it's hard to simply be still and know that He is God. So often we go to worship services and sing songs about how marvelous and wonderful He is, but when was the last time you truly marveled at Him? How often do you just stand in wonder of His greatness? If you're anything like me in college, then it's not often enough.

I will praise you; for I am fearfully and wonderfully made: marvelous are your works; and that my soul knows right well.

-Psalm 139:14

You've probably heard that verse before. I've heard numerous pastors preach on it, and while those sermons were good, they always focused on the first part. Now, we are all, without question, fearfully and wonderfully made. I mean just look at your hand for a second. Have you ever thought about its complexity? Did you know that each hand consists of twenty-seven bones? That means your hands constitute more than a quarter of the 206 bones in your entire body. And did you know that if you unwrap all the DNA you have in all your cells, you could reach the moon 6000 times? We have obviously been painstakingly constructed. But let's focus on the second half of the verse: "marvelous are your works; and that my soul knows right well."

We tend to treat a lot of the stuff we learn like "fun facts." I mean it's a fun fact to know that a giraffe's neck has the same number of vertebra in it as a human's does. That's an interesting thing to know. But have you ever just marveled at something like that? Do you stand in awe of the way your organs work together? Because it's truly an incredible system.

Yet, the psalmist goes a step further. He doesn't just marvel at how he's made; he says that even his soul—the fabric of his being—knows how great God's creation is. Now, I could make lists for days with all sorts of awe inspiring information, but would you just treat them as fun facts? Or would you marvel at them down to your soul?

In college, you get the incredible opportunity to learn about things most people don't even know exist. From the extraordinarily complex to the miraculously simple, you'll find out how phenomenal the universe is. Just don't forget to praise the God from which everything stems from.

For most people, we often marvel at the beauty of a sunrise or the magnificence of a full moon, but it is impossible to fathom the magnitude of the universe that surrounds us.

-Richard H. Baker

Fit

I realize that Americans aren't big on being under a king or ruler. This is the land of the free, home of the brave, and all that, and we don't like for anyone to control us. But do you realize that God is the Lord of lords and the King of kings? That He's the alpha and omega—the One who was and is and is to come—the glorious one—the Creator—the all-knowing, all-powerful, unstoppable force of the universe who spoke the stars into existence and holds time in the palm of his hand? Do you get that? More importantly, do you live like you get it?

God, the blessed and only Ruler, the King of kings and Lord of lords, who alone is immortal and who lives in unapproachable light, whom no one has seen or can see.

-1 Timothy 6:15-16

You see, a lot of Christians get to college, and they don't actually understand the magnitude of that verse. They may claim to, but their lifestyles will tell you otherwise. And the only explanation I can come up with is that these people don't actually know God. Because if you know God—if you're actually in a relationship with Him—then He is the number one priority in your life. Everything else is just secondary.

Yet, we try to find a place for *Him* in our busy schedules. Is that a joke? Is the Creator of the universe going to be satisfied at us penciling Him in for a couple hours a week? Give me a break. This is all or nothing. There's no such thing as a half-way Christian. You either love God or you don't. You're either seeking how to love Him better or you're not. It's that simple.

While the concept is easy, I understand how tough it can be to actually carry out. There are plenty of days when I don't particularly feel like loving God. I don't always see how He's working in my life. Sometimes I get so busy with stuff that I forget to stop and pray. Other times it's just inconvenient. But I move forward. It's just like any other relationship; if you really care about it, you'll put in the time.

So when I don't feel like loving Him or when it becomes inconvenient, I make it a point to do more than I normally would. If I don't feel like reading the Bible, I push myself to read an extra chapter. If I don't have time to pray, I slow down and make time. Not so I can be a good little Christian but because my relationship with God is important.

I hate Wednesdays. I don't know why, but Wednesday is just never a good day of the week for me. I'm always tired and rarely feel like doing anything. So when I had the opportunity to serve at a homeless shelter one day a week, I chose to go on Wednesdays. I refuse to let how I feel or how busy I am jeopardize my relationship with God. Not because I want to write about it in a book, but because it's the most valuable part of life.

It's not about asking God to come into your life. It's about fitting your life into Him.

So how does your life fit into God? Do you act like He's the Lord of lords and King of kings? Do you see Him as the blessed and only Ruler? Are you living as a subject in His kingdom? Or has God become a court jester in yours?

Worth

So why be a Christian at all? What person in his right mind would subject himself to such a lifestyle? Is it even worth it? Well, let me ask you a better question.

Do you realize how great God is?

When God made his promise to Abraham, since there was no one greater for Him to swear by, He swore by Himself

-Hebrews 6:13

He's so great that there is no greater force in the universe to swear by, so He has to swear by Himself. I love that. It makes me smile every time I think about it. Just think about how people would look at you if you started swearing by yourself. "I swear to Susan that I'll get to the movies on time." It just doesn't have the same ring to it.

I mean we're talking about God here—the Being who knew us before we were even born. He knows the number of hairs on our heads; He knows the desires of our hearts. And for some reason, He loved us enough to send His son to die for us. The almighty God thought that you and I were worth saving. He thought we were worth *His* time. Yet we have trouble deciding whether or not He's worth ours. That's a tragedy. His worth shouldn't even be an issue.

Make no mistake, He is the only thing that truly matters.

If you have not chosen the Kingdom of God, it will make in the end no difference what you have chosen instead. We shall have missed the end for which we are formed and rejected the only thing that satisfies. Does it matter to a man dying in the desert by which choice of route he missed the only well?

-C.S. Lewis

When it's all said and done, if you didn't think God was worth it, it won't matter what you chose instead. Sex, money, success, comfort—whatever it is you have chosen over God, it will lead to emptiness and the demolition of your soul. The Bible is pretty clear about that.

Enter through the narrow gate. For wide is the gate and broad is the road that leads to destruction, and many enter through it.

-Matthew 7:13

So what is God worth to you?

The kingdom of heaven is like treasure hidden in a field. When a man found it, he hid it again, and then in his joy went and sold all he had and bought that field.

-Matthew 13:44

Would you be willing to give up everything you own to have Him? Is He worth *that* much to you?

I remember being in a toy store when I was a kid, and I found this action figure that I really wanted. I didn't have enough money to buy it, and it was the only one left, so I hid it behind a bunch of girl toys. A week later, after I got my allowance, I went back to the store and bought the action figure.

Now, why would a ten year old do that? Because I thought it was important for me to have that toy. I didn't want anything to get in the way of me having it, so I hid it. In short, I treasured it; I was willing to do whatever it took to make sure I got it. Do you treasure God in the same way? Do you do everything you can to keep the rest of the world from taking Him away from you? Or do you know he's buried in the field but don't do anything about it?

It's so easy to let the world distract us from our relationship with God. I realize how busy college life is, and I know it's difficult to find time for Him. But if you truly care about your relationship with Him, you'll make time—not because you feel obligated, but because He is the most important aspect of your being. Trust me when I tell you He is *so* worth it.

There's not a thing on this planet worth more than an intimate relationship with God. He carved out the oceans. He set the galaxy in motion. And incredibly, He wants nothing more than to know you personally. But is that relationship worth it to you? Or is something else more important? Don't worry; over the next few years you'll have plenty of opportunities to prove how much you think He's worth.

2. Purpose

We are not primarily called to do something or go somewhere; we are called to Someone. We are not called first to special work but to God. The key to answering the call is to be devoted to no one and to nothing above God Himself.

-Os Guinness

I know a lot of people, many of them college students, who are desperately searching for purpose. Some have changed majors four times. Some are constantly attending career fairs. Some work crappy job after crappy job. Some even pray fervently for God to enlighten them on the purpose He has for their lives. So many people waste so much time searching for what to do in life. They keep hoping a booming voice from heaven will come down. And honestly, I just don't get it.

Love the Lord your God with all your heart, with all your soul, with all your mind, and with all your strength.

-Mark 12:30

Love your neighbor as yourself.

-Mark 12:31

That is our purpose. Love God. Love people. Period. It really is that simple.

Love

Love is the most powerful thing on earth. It's stronger than war, politics, disease, hunger, death, and every other evil of this world. It's even stronger than religion. Love is, without question, the driving force for good on this planet. Without it, we're screwed. With it, there is hope for a new day. It is truly the most central idea to the teachings of Christ, and if you discern only one thing from His life, make sure it's love.

Just read First Corinthians thirteen. Paul gets it. He never even met Jesus in the flesh and he gets it. Paul understands that a life without love is useless—it's a clanging cymbal; it's just a bunch of annoying noise.

Without love, a faith strong enough to move mountains means nothing. Think about that. If you don't love God and love people, it doesn't matter if you can tell Kilimanjaro to step aside; your life is still devoid of meaning.

So when you're searching for purpose, you have to start with love. It's the reason we're here. Everything we do should stem from it.

I've met a number of people who felt like their lives were meaningless. They were constantly looking for something of value—painstakingly probing their own lives and the lives of others trying to glean a reason to get out of bed. Some looked for ways to make more money. Some sought more fame. Some searched for intellectual enlightenment. None of them were seeking ways to love. And a lot of them were Christians. It's like we think it can't be that easy. Surely there's more to it than that. All I know is that the happiest people I've met are the ones who are constantly finding ways to serve and love others. And when you love others, you love God. Matthew 25:40. It says it right there.

I heard someone once say, "I wake up in the morning in order to find a reason to wake up in the morning." The reason you and I wake up each morning is in order to find more ways to love and care for other people. Don't overcomplicate it. Don't make it hard. Love God. Love people. That is our purpose. Now we just have to find ways to fulfill that purpose.

Vocation

Don't mistake vocation for purpose. A vocation is a job. It's a profession. It's not the main reason you're on the earth. You're probably going to have more jobs throughout your life than you can imagine. This isn't 1950. Times have changed. Gone are the days when people went to work at the same company doing the same job for forty years. Your career is going to be full of ups and downs. Just remember that a job is a means to an end. It's a vocation. It's not an end in itself. It's not your purpose.

I've met a couple people who are absolutely married to their jobs. I once knew a guy named Gavin who was completely engulfed by his profession. Now, Gavin was a Christian guy; he went to church on Sundays; he wasn't afraid to claim to be a Christian. But there were times when Gavin didn't treat people very well because of his job. When you become completely infatuated with what you do—when you lose sight of your purpose—when you forget the real reason you're here, you tend to start acting like the rest of the world. And that's what happened to Gavin.

He wanted to be successful; he wanted to make a lot of money; he wanted to prove his critics wrong; and to accomplish those things, "love God, love people" would have to fall by the wayside. So Gavin lied to people. He stopped caring about anyone who wasn't making him more successful. He became the typical businessman of today. And all the while he went to church and professed Christianity. As far as I know, Gavin is still living this way, and his life is a lie because of it. He's lost track of his purpose. He's abandoned love God, love people in favor of "success." He probably doesn't get much sleep.

You can't love people on your own terms. When you do that,

you become like Gavin. You put yourself before others and buy into what the world says is acceptable. The world will tell you that it's perfectly fine to put your career first. Stepping on others is just part of the game. And you're more than welcome to buy into that; but it's not at all what Jesus taught.

Christian Vocation

Don't fall into the Christian vocation trap. People that work for God, so to speak, can just as easily lose sight of their purpose. Now, you probably don't currently work for a church, but if you want to pursue Christ, you're going to have to get out of your dorm room and find a way to serve. So when I say "Christian vocation," I'm referring to the one day, one weekend, one week, or however long task that you set out to do that loves and helps other people. It might be a mission trip. It might be volunteering at a soup kitchen. It might be becoming a mentor for a middle-schooler. (You get the idea.)

Christians get trapped by Christian vocations in the same way they do by secular ones—by focusing on the means to an end and not the end itself. Os Guinness puts it perfectly: "We are not called first to special work but to God." When we go on mission trips or volunteer at homeless shelters, we get that warm, gooey feeling inside. That's natural. It's not a bad thing. But if we start pursuing that feeling and stop pursuing God, there's a huge problem. I call those people goo junkies. They go out and do great things in the name of God, but their real goal is to feel warm and gooey. They're addicted to the goo. So their lives become less about God and more about the goo.

To make matters worse, a lot of pastors and youth directors have become "goo dealers." In an effort to get more people to go on trips—to get you to serve others—they'll say things like, "It feels really good to help people in need." Then they throw in snorkeling, skiing, or an amusement park to sweeten the deal. No one wants to go do mission work if you can't get a little "me" time, right. Sure, I'll go pass out food for the homeless, but I better get at least two days at the beach.

Now, there's nothing wrong with feeling good about helping others and doing fun stuff along the way. The question is would you go on a trip if it made you feel like crap and all your time was spent serving others? How about if you had to sleep on the ground and not get enough to eat? What if everyone you love and care for would disown you for going? Would you still go then? Are you honestly willing to suffer as Jesus did?

In high school, I went on a bunch of trips with my youth group. We went to Washington D.C.; we went to New Orleans; we went to lots of great places. We helped homeless people; we worked on houses; we did lots of great things. But looking back I realize I wasn't pursuing Jesus in any of that. My friends went on the trip, so I went. My girlfriend went on the trip, so I went. I heard about all the fun things to do, so I went. I made those trips about me. And while people in need were being helped, I was missing the point entirely. Instead of "Love God, Love people," my priorities were "Love fun, Love me." The "mission" stuff was just something I had to do before I got to the fun part.

Maybe you experienced the same type of thing. I feel like it's a common issue for high school students today. Perhaps it's even understandable. (That's a topic for a different book.) But you're in college now. It's time to grow up. It's time to evolve. It's time to put down childish ways. It's time to embrace God's purpose for your life.

Love God. Love people.

Major Dilemma

There are few college students who *don't* struggle with choosing a major. Most take a long time to decide, and even more end up changing. I've known some to change so many times that they end up taking seven years to get an undergrad degree. So, what's the deal? Why is it so hard to figure out a major and then see it through to the end? Especially as Christians, why do we struggle to decide and waste so much time and money in the process? Perhaps it's because some of these things:

Your mom is kind of a liar. Yeah, I said it. Don't worry though; my mom was kind of a liar too. It's a common belief that to be a "good parent" you need to tell your kids that the sky is the limit. As long as they work hard and eat their vegetables, they can be anything they want. No profession is beyond their dreams. And while it's good to encourage your kids like that, it isn't the most practical advice. A lot of people get to college with unrealistic ideas about their talents and abilities, and they crash and burn because of it. I'm not saying your mother should have crushed your dreams, but we all need an honest perspective on what we're good at.

My former roommate was majoring in computer science. He loves computers; he's good at working on them; it was an obvious choice in majors. Like me, and probably like you, his mother had told him his entire life that he could do anything. But then he started taking programming classes. I don't know if you've ever taken any programming, but it's truly challenging work. You either have a knack for it, or you don't. And my friend found out that he just wasn't very good at it.

Assignments that should have taken a few hours would take an entire weekend. Now, I'll give him credit, he put in the effort to really figure it out. He talked to his professors; he tried to learn from people who had already taken the classes. But it just wasn't working. Yet, he kept thinking "I can do this. I can do anything." He kept taking the classes, and he managed to scrape by. But with every new assignment he got more and more frustrated. He lost more and more sleep. Each new project put him in a worse mood.

One day we were talking about it and I asked how many more programming classes he had to take. He looked it up and the list was rather discouraging. So I asked him, "Is this how you want to feel for the next three years?" He changed his major the next semester. So maybe his mother wasn't a liar; maybe he could have hung on and clawed his way to a degree in computer science. But at what cost? Instead he was honest with himself—honest about his abilities—and now he's in a better major and better mood because of it. It's not about something being too hard so you quit; it's about understanding what you're good at and then making good decisions based on that.

Or maybe your problem is that you're really good at a bunch of different things. Maybe God's blessed you with a ton of talents and abilities, and now you can't decide on just one to pursue. If that's the case, I encourage you to make a list of all the things you don't like. Write down all the things you're really bad at. It may seem useless, but it's amazing how many majors you can eliminate. But you have to be honest. This is no place for pride. My list looks like this:

Stuff I suck at/don't like:

Drawing	Computers
Cars	Agriculture
Math	Foreign Languages
Science	Politics
Music	Business

Just by being honest about myself I was able to cut out a giant percentage of possible majors. If you're unsure about a specific major, then take an entry level class and talk to people about to graduate in it. And if you're in a crappy major now don't be afraid to say, "You know what, this isn't working."

The most important thing you can do while choosing a major is pray. Ask for God to lead you to the right one. Once again, you have to be honest about this. You can't get mad if God sends you in a direction you don't want to go.

Whatever you ask in My name, I will do it so that the Father may be glorified in the Son.

-John 14:13

Remember that it's not about you. What you pursue in college should be for the glory of God—for the progression of His kingdom. Before you choose a major ask yourself "How will this major help me to love God and love people?" Your classes are where you lay the foundation for how to change the world. Everything you learn should bear that in mind. Don't memorize information to get a good grade; learn it so you can apply it to a real life situation.

One day, while working at a homeless shelter in Los Angeles, I met an optometrist. He brought a couple hundred pairs of reading glasses and examined people out of the back of his truck for hours. Because of him, a ton of people can now see clearly what was once blurry. He took what he had learned in school, and he used it to love people. And when you love the "least of these," you love God. Find a way to make what you learn in school relevant to your purpose, and give God the glory all the while.

A final note on majors: relax. You're not deciding on something that you'll be forced to do the rest of your life. Truth be told, most people get jobs that don't even pertain to their majors. What's important is that you go in the direction God leads you. So figure out what you're good at and pursue it.

Learn who you are and be such

-Pindar

To Hell with the American Dream

Let's get something straight: I love the United States of America. I love it. I played football in the SEC; my favorite food is a hamburger; I know all the words to the "Star Spangled Banner." I have a beard. I'm as American as they come. Yet, I can't help but recognize how anti-Christian the American dream is. It reminds me of a certain parable.

"The ground of a certain rich man produced a good crop. He thought to himself, 'What shall I do? I have no place to store my crops.'

"Then he said, 'This is what I'll do. I will tear down my barns and build bigger ones, and there I will store all my grain and my goods. And I'll say to myself, "You have plenty of good things laid up for many years. Take life easy; eat, drink and be merry." '

-Luke 12:16-19

Is that not the epitome of the American dream? Work hard, make a bunch of money, retire, and then take it easy; that's the definition of success here. It's what we're all supposed to be striving for. Instead of "how can I use this money to serve God," we ask "how can I earn more interest off this money and improve my 401k so I can be more comfortable?" "How can I build a bigger storehouse?" But that leads me to the best part of the story.

"But God said to him, 'You fool! This very night your life will be demanded from you. Then who will get what you have prepared for yourself?'

"This is how it will be with anyone who stores up things for himself but is not rich toward God."

-Luke 12:20-21

Wow. And if I'm not mistaken, this is the only parable Jesus tells in which the crime is so heinous that God actually takes a person's life. But why? That man didn't murder anybody; he didn't rape anyone. Truth be told, he did exactly what nearly everyone in this country would do. And God took his life. Why?

Because he was selfish.

He wasn't rich toward God. Instead of thanking God for such a blessing and then finding ways to bless others, he stored it all up. He decided to take life easy. If he had lived here, he would have been fulfilling the American dream. We would have all talked about what a huge success story he was. But that "success" got him killed.

It bothers me when someone says this is a "Christian country." That's garbage. How do I know? Simple. Just look at the most well-known part in what is probably the most well-known document about what we as Americans are guaranteed.

"We hold these truths to be self-evident, that all men are created equal, that they are endowed by their Creator with certain unalienable Rights, that among these are Life, Liberty and the *pursuit of Happiness*."

-The Declaration of Independence

This is a very interesting line because while it acknowledges a Creator, it also goes completely against the life and teachings of Christ. As Christians we don't pursue happiness. Our happiness be damned. We pursue Jesus to bring glory to God. We love Him and love people. Happiness is just a side effect. It's a byproduct of what we were put on this earth to do.

But that's not how most of us live is it? No, we like our stuff too much. We like our nice cars sitting outside our big houses in our safe neighborhoods. We like our white picket fences. We constantly pursue happiness and avoid anything that might jeopardize it. And if God can find a way to fit into that then so be it. But if He starts leaning on us—if He starts asking too much—then we'll just pick and choose verses out of the Bible to justify our lifestyles. We'll avoid all the ones that make us feel convicted; we'll pretend like those verses about how hard it is for rich men to get into heaven don't exist. Oh, and the ones about collecting the possessions of this world—they're gonna have to go too. Can't let anything get in the way of all this success and happiness, you know.

The more I read the Bible—the more I learn about Jesus and the early Christians—the more I can't help but realize how anti-Christ the American dream is.

People who want to get rich fall into temptation and a trap and into many foolish and harmful desires that plunge men into ruin and destruction.

-1 Timothy 6:9

Don't collect for yourselves treasures on earth, where moth and rust destroy and where thieves break in and steal.

-Matthew 6:19

Do not love the world or the things that belong to the world. If anyone loves the world, love for the Father is not in him.

-1 John 2:15

It just seems so obvious. Pursuing the riches and possessions of this world only leads to destruction. So here's the deal: you can't chase the American dream AND be a Christian. It's not possible. They are two completely opposite ideologies. One says take, take, take. The other says give, give, give. To put it simply: if you love what this country calls success—if your pursuit in life is money, comfort, and happiness—then the love for the Father is not in you.

If you want a religion to make you feel really comfortable, I certainly don't recommend Christianity.

-C.S. Lewis

I've talked to so many young people who don't yet know what career path to take, but they all usually end up saying the same thing: "I don't know what I want to do yet; I just want to make a lot of money." Now, don't get it twisted; money in itself is not a bad thing. Where we run into trouble is when it becomes a passion—when it becomes a main goal and priority.

I'm not saying you have to live in poverty to be a good Christian. There are plenty of people who God has blessed with plenty of money. You just have to realize what that money is for. If God blesses you with abundance it is so you can bless others abundantly.

If anyone has this world's goods and sees his brother in need but shuts off his compassion from him—how can God's love reside in him?

-1 John 3:17

We are judged not by how much we have but by how much we give. God doesn't bless you for you. It's not so you can build bigger storehouses; it's so you can help, love, and care for other people.

So why am I telling a college student all this? I mean you're probably struggling just to buy books every semester, and there's a good chance you're living off ramen noodles and the value menu. I'm telling you because college is when you decide which path in life to take. College is your best opportunity to figure out what you're good at and what you're passionate about, and too many Christians forgo their passion in the pursuit of money.

A couple years ago, when some people in my family found out I was majoring in English, they questioned what I was going to do with that type of degree. I didn't really know at the time; all I knew was that I enjoyed writing and that I had a passion for reading and telling good stories. But to avoid a long, drawn out conversation, I gave the cliché answers that I was thinking about law school or possibly becoming a teacher.

The next ten minutes was filled with conversation about how getting a teaching certificate was a terrible idea. Not because being a good teacher is hard or because dealing with kids all day can cause bouts of insanity, they didn't want me to become a teacher because that profession doesn't make any money. And if I don't make enough money, it's going to be really hard to be happy. Wow. Really? So if I have an extraordinary teaching ability and God has blessed me with that passion, then I should tell God to go screw himself in favor of a higher paying job. Yeah, that sounds like a great idea. That's definitely something I want to account for when I get to heaven…

Jesus: Welcome to the afterlife.

Me: It's good to be here.

Jesus: You did pretty well for yourself. Made a lot of money I see.

Me: Yeah. Couldn't have lived like that without money.

Jesus: It says here you became an investment banker[1]. What happened to all that passion and ability I gave you?

Me: Well, I took it all into account and decided that passion and ability weren't going to buy all the shiny things I wanted.

Jesus: So, it seems you chose to pursue wealth instead of Me.

Me: Uh, yeah…I guess I did.

Jesus: Interesting. Now, what did you say your name was again?

Me: Gabe. Why?

Jesus: Hmm. It would appear I never knew you.

Me: Uh oh.

That's just not how I want it to go down. But if you're cool with spitting in God's face and pursuing money over Him, then have fun. Just let me remind you of one important fact:

[W]e brought nothing into the world, and we can take nothing out.

-1 Timothy 6:7

Remember *that* before you start chasing the American dream. Money is nice and having a ton of it will definitely make your life more comfortable. But what's more important to you: money or Jesus?

What good is it for a man to gain the whole world, yet forfeit his soul?

-Mark 8:36

I want to end this section by passing along a challenge from Francis Chan. In a short video on Youtube, Francis points out a section of Proverbs:

Two things I ask of you, O LORD; do not refuse me before I die: Keep falsehood and lies far from me; give me neither poverty nor riches, but give me only my daily bread. Otherwise, I may have too much and disown you and say, 'Who is the LORD?' Or I may become poor and steal and so dishonor the name of my God

-Proverbs 30:7-9

That's a pretty intense prayer. The question is: Do you have the guts to pray that? Do you trust God enough to ask Him to only grant you your daily bread? Do you love Him more than the pursuit of wealth? Jesus said it pretty well:

No one can serve two masters. For you will hate one and love the other; you will be devoted to one and despise the other. You cannot serve both God and money.

-Matthew 6:24

I hope you love God more than the American dream. I pray that you will seek to fulfill His purpose for your life and give up the pursuit for worldly "success."

Be Inspired by True Events

I have a friend named Katie. She's one of those people that the more you spend time with, the more you realize how little you're doing for the world. She doesn't beat you over the head with a Bible or make you feel guilty or anything; she just tells story after story of how God is working in other parts of the planet.

I met Katie in college right before she went on a mission trip to Kenya. She was already majoring in journalism, but this life changing trip showed her exactly what kind of writing she wanted to pursue. During the next summer, she interned at a major home decorating magazine, but it just wasn't the right fit for her. In Kenya, God had revealed her passion. The magazine internship simply paled in comparison.

Right before she graduated, a job opportunity appeared out of nowhere. When I asked about it she said, "I honestly didn't look for this. It just happened. It felt right, like Southeast Asia was where I was supposed to be. And it is." I love that. Katie wasn't pursuing a job; she was pursuing God. And when you pursue God, He puts you where you need to be. Now she gets to travel to other countries as a writer and photographer to cover stories about missionaries. On a daily basis, she gets to write about how God is interacting with people in parts of the world I didn't even know existed.

Katie shared one of her favorite verses with me.

You will seek and find Me when you seek with all your heart.

-Jeremiah 29:13

Katie gets it. She's not buying in to the American dream. She realizes there's a lot more to life than what's in her bank account. She tells me, "God promised to be there if we only look, and in looking, we fulfill our purpose." It's about living as He lived— walking as He walked.

A while back I read a post on Katie's blog that perfectly exemplifies her faith and character. I want to share it with you:

Through My Entire Lack of Linguistic Competence, He is Made Strong

Have you ever felt that God uses you more when you're a complete idiot – like He waits for you to have an exceptionally incompetent moment to work a miracle just to prove that you had nothing to do with it?

He does that to me.

About once a week my friends and I hold a Bible study with some of our Buddhist friends. We tell them about God and how He works in our lives – or we try to. None of us have a 3-year-old's grasp on the language, so we stumble through an English/local language hybrid, trying desperately to explain exactly who the Father is.

A couple weeks ago, we held a session with two Buddhist friends that was especially bad. Awkward Turtle bad. We talked about sin and how Christ died to pay for it but the concepts were too complex for our vocabularies. It's hard to explain the grace of God when your conversation capacity barely extends past "Where's the bathroom?" and "I'm from Kentucky – as in Kentucky Fried Chicken." God is way more complicated than chicken.

They knew some English, and we gave them translated versions of the Bible, but the explanations took a long, long time. It got to a point where I prayed, "God, if they come to faith tonight, it's definitely not going to be because of anything we did."

And, of course, they both became believers. I guess God wanted to make sure He got the credit. I like it that way, though. Humbling as it may be, God's

29

method reminds me that He's in control and I operate by His strength alone. I need the reminder pretty often.

I bet He also thinks it's funny.

Now, this isn't some made up story to inspire you. It's not some metaphor on what it would look like to follow Jesus. Katie is a real person. She's barely older than you are, and she's already doing great things for the kingdom of God. So what's holding you back? What's keeping you from a faith that's as strong as hers? What are you afraid of?

I met a guy named Greg a while back. We had a five minute conversation, and there's a good chance I'll never see him again. You see, when I talked to him, Greg was about to leave for Uganda. This was a little strange because we were right in the middle of a semester. When I asked him about the timing, he said he had dropped out a week ago. He didn't see any point in just riding it out. He knew what God wanted him to do, so he wasn't going to waste any time doing it. When I asked if he was going to come back and graduate he replied, "I don't know." I love that. It wasn't an "I don't know" of uncertainty; he simply didn't care. It wasn't up to him. Greg had placed his trust in God. He was going to get on a plane to Uganda, and let the Lord take it from there.

Have you ever talked to someone right after he gets engaged? No matter what he says, he has a huge smile on his face. This is how Greg was. It was like he had just realized his love for God, had gotten engaged, and was leaving for the wedding in Africa. Walt Whitman would have called him "so much sunshine to the square inch." And the best part about it is that Greg had no clue what was going to happen next. At twenty years old, he was moving from Alabama to Uganda. Now, that's faith worth talking about.

So, don't give me any garbage about age. You either love God or you don't. You're either actively seeking Him or you're not. I hope you have enough faith to say to God, "Your will be done." If you don't, you need to really start praying for more opportunities to grow. You need to dig into the Bible and learn how Jesus did it. Then, emulate Him. (More to come on that.)

If your faith is strong enough to say "Your will over my will," and nothing has come along yet, be patient. Just keep knocking; the door will eventually be opened to you.

May you fulfill God's purpose for your life. May you do it with a trusting spirit and indomitable will. May you be a world changer from a young age.

Don't ask what the world needs. Ask what makes you come alive, and go do it. Because what the world needs is people who have come alive.

-Howard Thurman

3. Daily Life

Death is always on the way, but the fact that you don't know when it will arrive seems to take away from the finiteness of life. It's that terrible precision that we hate so much. But because we don't know, we get to think of life as an inexhaustible well. Yet everything happens a certain number of times, and a very small number, really. How many more times will you remember a certain afternoon of your childhood, some afternoon that's so deeply a part of your being that you can't even conceive of your life without it? Perhaps four or five times more. Perhaps not even. How many more times will you watch the full moon rise? Perhaps twenty. And yet it all seems limitless.

— Paul Bowles

Most of what you'll remember about college will be big events. A certain party; a first kiss; a research project; an enlightening conversation; and so on. And while those things are important, they're not nearly as significant as everyday life. Why? Because what you do during the mundane, forgettable time of daily college life is going to determine how you react during the big, pivotal moments that you'll be telling your grandkids about.

Here's the deal: Christianity is a choice. And it's a choice you make every single day. God has blessed us with the wonderful ability to choose, and every day comes with the choice to either love Him or hate Him. There is no "liking" God; He doesn't give us that option. And on a daily basis you'll have the opportunity to prove which side you're on. You may have confessed Jesus to be your Lord and Savior. You may claim to love God with all your heart. But what does your everyday life say?

The You-niversity

College is about you. That's how it's been designed. That's how the system has been set up. You're supposed to figure out which direction to take your life, who you want to be, what kind of job you want, who you want to hang around, where you want to go, what you want to believe, and possibly even who you want to spend the rest of your life with. You're expected and encouraged to make the next four years about *you*. It's the "You-niversity". But buying into that is a load of crap.

You're gonna have to fight to not become self-absorbed in college. And trust me, it's a struggle. My friend Jenny was planning on spending spring break in South America on a mission trip. While most people would be in Florida staying in nice hotels and hanging out on the beach all day, she would be living in a wooden shack with no running water and hanging out with people who barely spoke English. When she told her dad about the trip he asked, "Shouldn't you be worrying about your own stuff instead of going to some other country?"

Now, this was a Christian guy asking his daughter a very reasonable question. He wanted what was best for her and didn't think a trip to a third world country was going to help her accomplish her goals in life. Fair enough. But he was also perpetuating the lie that college should be about *you*. I've been told of numerous parents telling their kids to focus on themselves during college and then start worrying about other people once they graduate. In other words, devote four or five years to yourself and pretend like you'll be able to flip the switch one day to start thinking about others. Not to say it isn't possible to go from completely selfish to completely giving, but if you go through your entire college career and focus mainly on yourself, you're going to create some really nasty habits that will be difficult to overcome.

Think of it this way: A carpenter builds nothing but barns for four years. Then, one day someone asks him to build a house. So he does. But it takes him twice as long as it should, and the house ends up looking a lot like a barn.

Excellence is an art won by training and habituation. We do not act rightly because we *have* virtue or excellence, but we rather have those because we have acted rightly. We are what we repeatedly do. Excellence, then, is not an act but a habit

-Aristotle

Aristotle wasn't even close to being a Christian, but he gets it. To achieve greatness, you have to practice it every day. To become more like Jesus, you have to live it out every single day. Love and kindness should be habits. They should be so ingrained in you that they come out before you even have a chance to think. It's like muscle memory. If you show them repeatedly, love and kindness become second nature.

Spending four years as a selfish college student won't make you inept at helping other people. You won't lose the ability. But devoting so much time to yourself usually leads to acts of kindness that are self-serving. Reaching out to others will be fueled by selfish motives. And it won't necessarily be intentional; it's just a habit. Selflessness is a skill. And like any other skill, if you don't do it often, you won't be very good at it. You can't show up to the game without practicing and expect to win.

Let's go back to my friend Jenny. In spite of her dad's wishes, she went to South America on spring break. She decided to deny the lie of the You-Niversity. She knew that God had not put her here to be served. He placed her on this planet to serve others. And the same goes for you and me.

Now, avoiding the self-absorbed college life doesn't mean

you have to run off to other countries. You don't have to beat people over the head with a Bible. You don't have to wear cheesy Christian t-shirts. You don't even have to pray really loudly before you eat in the cafeteria. You simply have to start putting yourself second. Start slow; start small. Putting others first goes completely against human nature and takes a lifetime to master. Don't get discouraged when it takes a while. The important thing is that you don't wait four or five years to get started.

So why not today? Be honest. What's stopping you?

Everyday Christianity

Christianity is moment to moment. We look forward to eternity, but until then, we're commanded to live day to day.

Therefore do not worry about tomorrow, for tomorrow will worry about itself. Each day has enough trouble of its own.

-Matthew 6:34

Does that mean you don't plan for the future? Of course not. It just means we shouldn't be anxious about tomorrow. Live each moment like it's your last. You never know when it will be.

You don't even know what tomorrow will bring—what your life will be. You are a mist that appears for a little while and then vanishes.

-James 4:14

We're all living on borrowed time—merely waves of mist

ready to vanish—with no guarantees about what tomorrow will hold. Putting something off for another day could mean putting it off permanently. Now, I don't want you to live in *fear* that today might be your last. I just want you to be aware of it. I spent roughly 1700 days as a college student, but not a single one was promised to me. Realize that every day you roll out of bed, you're staring death in the face. But don't just realize it; live like it. Live in a way that when you open your eyes each morning, the Devil starts cussing because you're awake.

But how do you do that? How do you live in a way that pisses Satan off?

Prayer

Devote yourselves to prayer, being watchful and thankful.

-Colossians 4:2

Your relationship with God **has** to start with prayer. Just like any other relationship, you have to communicate, and prayer is the best way to communicate with God. However, there are some misconceptions about talking to the Father.

Prayer is not about giving God a grocery list of everything you want and need.

And when you pray, do not keep on babbling like pagans, for they think they will be heard because of their many words. Do not be like them, for your Father knows what you need before you ask Him.

-Matthew 6:7-8

We serve an all-knowing God. He is fully aware of what you want and need; He knows before you do. And while it's important to petition God for things we want to happen, think of it more as a time to be still and listen to Him. We rarely stop and take time to just listen to God, but that's exactly what prayer should be.

When you have a problem, you talk to an expert. You find someone who knows more about the problem than you do and who knows how to fix it. And if you're smart, you listen to the expert and let him fix it. Yet, with God, we have a tendency to talk too much and pray and pray and pray without actually listening to Him. He's telling us answers, but we don't hear Him because we're still talking. So when you pray, talk less and listen more. Clear your mind and put the ball in His court. You might be surprised by what you hear.

You ask and don't receive because you ask wrongly, so that you may spend it on your desires for pleasure.

-James 4:3

God hears all prayers; but he does not listen to all of them. I mean would you? Thinking back over some of my prayers from the last few years, I'm thankful God didn't listen. There's a lot of things I'm glad He let slide. It wasn't until recently that I truly understood the actual purpose of prayer.

Prayer is about lining up your will with God's will. It's less about asking Him to fulfill needs and more about abandoning your pride to say you need them. It's less about asking for wants and more about seeking what God wants. When God answers a prayer, it isn't because it's what *you* wanted; it's because He wanted it. So when your prayers come to fruition, it means your will and His will are one in the same.

Pray daily. Don't just rush through it. Relax. Think about what you're going to say. Say it. And then listen. You're talking to the most high God here. Think of it that way. And I dare you to pray what Jesus prayed.

Yet not my will but yours be done.

-Luke 22:42

The Bible

A while back I realized God isn't wanting me to read the Bible as much as He's wanting me to *want* to read the Bible. So often we look at the words, but we don't see them. There have been times when I've read entire chapters only to get to the end and not remember what I read. That's a waste of time. Going through the motions and reading the Bible because you're "supposed" to is useless. If you don't take something away from what you read, then why read it? It's not all going to make sense. There are going to be plenty of times when you'll need a more detailed explanation for you to understand what's going on.

The point is that you're actually seeking God. You read the Bible to get a better idea about what God is like. You read the words in red to figure out how to live and walk as Jesus did. The Bible should be the most cherished book in your possession because when you get right down to it, it's the only one that actually matters. Let me ask you this: If the government took every Bible in the entire country and burned them, would that change your life at all? Sure, it would piss you off that the government would do such a thing, but would it bother you that you didn't have a Bible to read anymore?

All Scripture is God-breathed and is useful for teaching, rebuking, correcting and training in righteousness, so that the man of God may be thoroughly equipped for every good work.

-2 Timothy 3:16-17

Do you treat the Bible like it's God-breathed? Or is it just a book? Are you using it to become better equipped for life? Or do you treat it like an irrelevant piece of old literature?

I hope you see the Bible's importance. I pray you cherish it as the living word of God. If you're having trouble finding time to read it, **then make time**. It's one of the most important things you can do each day. And if you want your relationship with God to grow deeper, you have to read and study His word. But don't just read it; **do what it says**. Set a time every day to read the Bible. It might be when you first wake up; it might be during lunch. Whenever it is, stick to it. It should be just as important to you as eating. Without food, you can't live physically. Without the Bible, you can't live spiritually. It's that simple.

Jesus answered, "It is written: 'Man does not live on bread alone, but on every word that comes from the mouth of God.'"

-Matthew 4:4

Worship

Jesus answered, "It is written: 'Worship the Lord your God and serve him only.'"

-Luke 4:8

Worship plays a huge role in our relationships with God. It's the dividing line between a God-centered life and a self-centered life. To truly worship God is to realize that He is the most important part of life, and that we can't make it without Him. We praise and honor Him because we realize how much He deserves it. We worship Him through prayer, through song, and through how we live our lives.

Once again, don't make prayer all about you. Pray in a way that worships God. Don't just ask Him for what you need; thank Him for being part of your life. Praise Him for being the awe-inspiring creator of the universe. Compliment His timing. Bless Him for blessing you.

Go to a worship service once a week. It's important to find a place where you can worship God with other Christians. Most campuses have groups that meet on Wednesday or Thursday nights; seek them out. (There might even be food there.)

[W]hether you eat or drink, or whatever you do, do everything for God's glory.

-1 Corinthians 10:31

Your everyday life should worship God. No matter what you're doing, keep God in mind. It's really easy to lose focus and start worshiping things other than God. Basically, it comes down to this: Tell me where your time and money go and I'll tell you what you worship. How you handle those two things shows what you love and care about. And it's either God's kingdom or your own.

So what do you worship? Be honest. Is it success? Sports? A relationship? Fame? Sex? Yourself? Or are you truly seeking God's glory in everything you do? Do your time and money prove that?

Church

It is imperative that you find a church to be a part of while you're off at school. Notice I didn't say find a church *to go to*. Going to a building and calling it church is only an empty shell of the real thing. You need to find a group of Christians that you can share your trials and triumphs with. You need to find people that you actually care about and who genuinely care about you. If they happen to meet in a building on Sunday mornings, then great. Just remember that the church is made of people, not bricks and mortar.

Getting connected with a group of Christians will keep you in the loop of the needs and struggles where you live. Campus often becomes its own little gated community, and it's easy for the problems off campus to go unnoticed. Being involved with a church will put you around people who are encountering all sorts of issues. Just hanging around these people will cause you to grow up as a person, and it will better your relationship with God.

So look around. Visit a bunch of different churches before deciding to be a part of one. It shouldn't be a decision you take lightly. Find a place where you fit them and they fit you. Then get involved. Don't assume someone's going to ask you to do something. Seek out opportunities. Find out when they have Bible studies; get the times on worship services; learn about all the ways they're helping in the community. And then go do those things. Don't be just another random college student taking up space on a pew.

I cannot overstress how important it is for you to find a good church home while you're in college. It should be one of the first things you look for when you get there.

Service

The greatest among you will be your servant. For whoever exalts himself will be humbled, and whoever humbles himself will be exalted.

-Matthew 23:11-12

It's interesting how Jesus came to be a servant. The King of kings and Lord of lords humbled himself and came to serve us.

He came to wash His disciples' feet. And we look at that in amazement, and we see how incredible that image is, but then we expect for someone else to scrub between *our* toes.

Make no mistake, God put you here to be a servant. You're not here to be served by someone else. And it's not a once a summer thing; it's not a weekend thing. Every single one of us was placed on this planet to serve on a daily basis. The opportunities are all around you, but do you see them? Think about all the interactions you have with people in a day. Do those exchanges bring heaven or hell into those people's lives? It's one or the other. I mentioned worship earlier, but do you realize how you treat people is an act of worship? In every conversation you're either glorifying God or you're glorifying yourself. You're worshiping Him or worshiping your own selfish motives. That doesn't mean every time you open your mouth Bible verses have to fall out. You can show someone Jesus without ever even mentioning His name. All it takes is having a genuine concern for the well-being of the people around you. That means having a heart for servanthood.

If you see a giant branch fall into the street, why not move it to make sure no one runs over it? If you see some people unloading a moving truck, why not go give them a hand? If you know a person is struggling, why not invite him over for dinner? Chances to serve are everywhere. Keep your head on a swivel. And when you see a need, fill it. It doesn't have to be big; it's often the little things that matter most.

When a poor person dies of hunger, it has not happened because God did not take care of him or her. It has happened because neither you nor I wanted to give that person what he or she needed.

-Mother Teresa

Hopefully, you read the Bible regularly. Perhaps you even go to a Bible study once a week. But what if you started a Bible practice? What if you took what you read and stopped talking about what it would look like to live like Jesus did and you started actually following through on it? "Love your neighbor as yourself." That's as plain as it can be. But are you doing that? On a daily basis, do you set out to do for others as much as you do for yourself? Are you really and truly pursuing a life of servanthood?

Character

Character is doing what's right because it's right. It's not about behaving or being a "nice" person; those are words our society and culture use. Your character should have nothing to do with what our society and culture think. (That's called Relativism.) Your character is based solely on doing what God says is right.

Character is one of the most important factors in changing the world for the better. It sits at the core of opening people's hearts to God. Without character, it doesn't matter what you say; it doesn't matter what you do; a person's heart will not be changed. Why would it? Why would anyone listen to you if your character shows you to be a liar and a crook? Why would a non-Christian listen to a Christian when they share the same character?

Your character is at the center of your ministry. Words and deeds bring people to you; your character proves your faith to be legitimate. It solidifies your message.

The true measure of a man is how he treats someone who can do him absolutely no good.

-Esther Pauline Friedman

On a daily basis, character is built on how you treat other people and the choices you make. Every interaction you have with someone else and every choice you make will either add or subtract from your character.

Tough times don't build character; they reveal it. When your life hits a wall and everything goes to hell in a hand basket, your character shines through. And it's how you've been dealing with life on a daily basis that will determine how you react in a crappy situation.

College is quite possibly the most important time for character. During these next few years, you'll have more chances to develop character than any other time in your life. The choices you make now will lay the foundation for your character for the rest of your time spent on earth.

So, guard your character.

I'm all about hanging out with non-Christians. It was a big part of Jesus' life, so it's been a big part of mine. However, there have been times when my character has started to suffer because of it. When that happened, I had to limit how much time I spent around those people because they were pulling my character down. There will be times when you'll have to do the same thing. Don't assume your character is going to pull people up to your level; it's actually easier for them to pull you down to theirs. And when it happens, you need to be honest about it and change what you're doing. Protect your character; it's important.

Rome wasn't built in a day. Neither is your character. It's a gradual and continuous process. But it never stays the same. You're either getting better or you're getting worse. You're either becoming more like Christ or you're becoming more like the world. And it all comes down to daily choices.

It's extraordinarily easy to cheat in college. I was actually surprised with how widespread it is and how simple it is to get away with. In a class with a hundred people where everyone is sitting right next to each other, it's not hard at all to glance over at your neighbor's test. It's not hard to find papers on the internet that can easily be copied and pasted into your own work. And the list goes on and on. Just remember that good character is better than a good grade. Character is doing what's right for the simple reason that it's right. If you're compromising your character now over something as small as a quiz or term paper, then what kind of choices are you gonna make down the road when the stakes are a lot higher?

Don't forget that Rome didn't crumble in a day either. It was a slow process over the course of a number of years that led to its downfall; and the same thing goes for your character. The choices you make on an everyday basis determine your eventual rise or fall.

Your character should have love at its core.

The one who does not love does not know God, because God is love

-1 John 4:8

Once again, we arrive back at love. And without love, good character is useless because it means you don't know God. There are plenty of people who possess incredible character, but it doesn't matter because they don't know God. Hell is full of people who never lied, cheated, or stole; they had character oozing out of their ears, but it was for nothing because they didn't know Jesus. So how do you make Jesus part of your character? You start by doing what's right because it's right in every facet of life. Then, you seek out the least of these and find ways to genuinely love and care for them.

But what if you already have really good character? What if you're at the top of your game? Well, in that case:

If you do things well, do them better.

-Anita Roddick

Get better. This isn't a case where you get to a certain point and then take it easy. There's no mark you're trying to reach. Your character can always improve; you can always find new ways to show love.

And if a certain part of your character isn't where you want it to be, pray about it. Ask God to send opportunities to get better. But you have to realize that your character and who you are is more important than where you are and what you're going through. Life isn't about what happens to you; it's about how you react to it. God is less concerned with changing your circumstances and more concerned with changing you. If you need more patience, God isn't going to just give it to you. You won't wake up one day as a more patient person. What He'll do is place you in situations around certain people that will test your patience. So don't ask God to remove the circumstances; ask Him to improve how you react to them.

Your character is extremely important. Throwing it away in college will set you up for tragic failure in life. However, doing what's right because it's right will put you in the position to do some awesome things for God.

Behaving

Let me make something extraordinarily clear: Christianity has nothing to do with behaving or being nice.

We must not suppose that if we succeeded in making everyone nice we should have saved their souls. A world of nice people, content in their own niceness, looking no further, turned away from God, would be just as desperately in need of salvation as a miserable world.

-C.S. Lewis

We need to get away from the idea that Christianity is about behaving. We've concocted this notion that if we are just really, really nice to people, that will somehow make us good Christians. Think about it. Why do you think religion so often comes with a long list of rules. Do these things; don't do those things; be a nice person; and then you'll go to heaven. But this is completely different that what Jesus taught. He didn't fill up people's lives with petty rules. He said love God; love people. If you follow those commands, everything will take care of itself.

Jesus didn't come all the way to Earth just to tell us to behave. I mean think about that for a second. What if He had stood in front of one of those large crowds and said, "Alright now guys, you need to start being a little nicer to each other, mmkay." That's not exactly earth-shattering. When someone is supposed to be the messiah—the savior of mankind—you hope he has something a little more riveting than "be nice."

And Jesus did.

He redefined the relationship with God. He redefined the relationship with other people. He changed everything. Suddenly, getting closer to God wasn't based on rules and regulations. It wasn't about dos and don'ts. It was about love[2]. And love is rarely "nice."

It's not very nice to confront a friend about a drug problem. It's not nice to talk to a roommate about watching porn three hours a day. It's not nice when God allows you to travel through the valley of the shadow of death.

It's all about love.

If you love your friend, you won't let her destroy her body with narcotics. If you love your roommate, you won't let him erode his brain with pornography. And it's out of love that God lets you come under trial and hardship.

I just don't see Jesus as a very "nice" person. Think about all the interactions people had with Jesus. Think about His conversations with the Pharisees. Think about the times when people came to Him seeking healing. Think about the times when people just "happened" to cross paths with Him. Now think about what they all said right after their interactions with Jesus. I doubt it was anything like, "Wow, that Jesus guy sure was swell."

Now, I'm not telling you to be a jerk or anything. What I'm saying is don't confuse Christianity with Moralism. Cleaning up your act and becoming a moral person has nothing to do with your soul. Behaving morally is just an imaginary way to justify your "goodness." And when you're a good person it's really easy to look at the world and think how righteous you are. But don't look at the people around you; compare yourself to God.

All of us have become like one who is unclean, and all our righteous acts are like filthy rags; we all shrivel up like a leaf, and like the wind our sins sweep us away.

-Isaiah 64:6

Compared to a holy God, we all fall short of righteousness. And the only way to rectify that is not by behaving but by establishing a relationship with Jesus. Without that relationship, you can be a good person all you want; it's not going to matter. To be frank, Hell is full of some extraordinarily nice people—folks who went to church every Sunday, went bowling with their youth groups, and went to Bible studies on Wednesday nights. Way too many people have said all the right things and put on a great show only to wind up before Jesus and have Him say, "I never knew you." I'm not saying this to scare you. The last thing I want to do is frighten someone to Christ. I just want you to know all the facts.

Matthew 7:14 is a fact.

So don't fall into the trap of Moralism. Christianity isn't about being "good." It's about Jesus. It's about having a genuine love for God and people.

Just remember: Jesus didn't come to make bad people good. He came to seek and save what was lost; He came to make dead people live.

Fishbowl Faith

I just finished reading a book from this same genre of Christianity in college. And while the author's heart was in the right spot, he ended up promoting a very rainbows and butterflies type of Christianity. He said to live in a bubble—a tremendous, perfect, Christian bubble. Don't go to parties. Don't you dare drink alcohol. If you listen to any music other than hymns, you don't love Jesus. Living in the dorm is evil; you should live at home to stay a good Christian. If someone starts to tell a dirty joke you need to run away as quickly as possible. If a professor ever mentions the word "evolution" you need to stick your fingers in your ears and say la, la, la.

Now, while this guy's philosophy on college isn't necessarily wrong, it doesn't really work. Like so many other authors on this subject, he is extremely afraid that you will lose your faith in college. So to keep you from turning away from God, he wants you to avoid absolutely anything that could introduce doubt into your mind. He's promoting a fishbowl Christianity. To be a good Christian you have to stay in your fishbowl. Feel free to look through the glass at the outside world, but you should never even think about leaving the bowl.

The bowl is safe. The bowl is comfortable. The bowl has everything a good Christian should want. To stay in the bowl is to live a life completely devoid of risk. Just bide your time; as long as you stay in the bowl, try to be a good person, and believe there's a God, you'll go to heaven.

This idea—this fishbowl Christianity—has become extremely popular in our country, but it is in direct conflict with the life of Christ and every book in the New Testament.

For it has been given to you on Christ's behalf not only to believe in Him, but also to suffer for Him.

-Philippians 1:29

I don't particularly like referring to Christians as "believers." Using the word isn't wrong; it just doesn't encompass what it truly means to be a Christ follower. For one thing, believing in God or in Christ doesn't make you a Christian. That's like saying believing in the wind makes you a meteorologist. I mean Satan himself believes there is a God; he knows Jesus came to save the world. And Satan has a much better understanding of God's power, ability, and existence than anyone you or I know. Satan knows what Jesus is capable of—what kind of influence the Holy Spirit can have. He's seen it all first hand. Does that make Satan a believer?

You believe that there is one God. Good! Even the demons believe that—and shudder.

-James 2:19

I don't like the word believer because Christianity is about a lot more than just what you believe. It's about what you live. It's one thing to believe Jesus is the way, the truth, and the life; it's a completely different thing to live it. Believing something doesn't come with as much risk. It doesn't come with suffering. The Bible is clear. To truly be a Christ follower requires more than just believing; you have to pick up a cross and follow after the one you believe in.

John 3:16 is arguably the most popular verse in the Bible. Even non-Christians can quote it word for word. It's like our go-to scripture.

For God so loved the world that he gave His one and only Son, that whoever believes in Him shall not perish but have eternal life.

-John 3:16

Now, I love this verse. It's beautiful. It brings hope to a dying, wretched world. But it is also being used to rationalize a fishbowl faith. We lift it up like it's more important than other verses in the Bible because it helps us justify our aversion to suffering. And if this were the only line of scripture we had to go on, then yes, merely believing in Jesus would be valid. But looking at scripture in its entirety shows that fishbowl Christianity goes completely against both the life of Christ and the teaching of the early church.

Somewhere along the line we took the idea of "being in the world but not of it" one step too far. As Christians, we stopped being in the world at all. We stopped being counter-cultural and became sub-cultural. In this country, we've convinced people to just leave us alone and let us have our own books, our own music, our own beliefs, our own TV, and our own communities. That way everybody's happy; no one has to feel uncomfortable; and most importantly, we don't have to suffer.

The Devil is using our freedom against us. Since we aren't

persecuted in this country like the people in the early church, we assume that those days are over. No one in the US of A is getting beheaded for being a Christian, so that suffering stuff must be over with. We're allowing ourselves to be lulled to sleep.

Whoever finds his *life* will *lose* it, and whoever loses his *life* for my sake will find it.

-Matthew 10:39

That verse doesn't necessarily mean death of your physical body. With some people, that's the case. But more often than not, especially here and now, that verse means giving up what *we* want out of life and submitting to what God wants. We lose our lives to Him. And in doing so, we find lives of actual value.

So how do you lose your life to God? You pursue His ultimate purpose for your life: to love Him and to love people. You avoid the fishbowl no matter what it costs. The bowl only has enough room for you and your belief in Jesus. Other people and a life that actually walks the path of Jesus just won't fit. To truly fulfill God's commands and purpose for your life, you are going to have to go out and be in the world but not of it. You are going to have to take on suffering and give up your life for a higher purpose. Why? Because Jesus is worth it. As Christians, we don't stockpile the treasures of this world; we seek our reward in heaven.

Do you remember the "Parable of the Talents" in Matthew 25? It's the one where the master leaves for a journey and gives three servants a different number of talents (money) to invest while he's gone. So the first two servants take their talents and invest them and double their money while the third servant buries his talent in the ground. Then the master returns and praises the first two servants for being faithful, and he casts out the third servant for being lazy and afraid. Which servant are you?

Are you going out and investing your talents in the world? Or have you buried your talent in your fishbowl? The Bible is pretty clear about which one Jesus prefers.

God didn't bless you for *you*. He didn't give you all that ability, talent, and skill just so you could feel really good about yourself. He didn't mean for you to use it to bless yourself. He gave it to you so you could go out and bless other people. If you're a good cook, then go volunteer at a soup kitchen. If you're really good with kids, then go babysit for a single mom while she goes to the grocery store. If you're really savvy with computers, then go fix a stranger's laptop. If you're really good at a particular subject, then go tutor someone who's struggling. This is not a hard concept. Whatever God has blessed you with the talent to do, go use it to bless someone else.

Don't live in a fishbowl; don't bury your talent and keep it to yourself. That's the opposite of Christianity. If you want Jesus to call you a "good and faithful servant," you're going to have to get out in the world and change it for the better.

Follow Me

"Come, follow Me," Jesus said, "and I will make you fishers of men." At once they left their nets and followed Him.

-Mark 1:17-18

Have you ever wondered why the disciples just dropped everything and followed Jesus? I mean if some dude showed up at your job and said, "Drop everything and let's go," would you immediately take off your name tag and peace out? Most people wouldn't. They would call security and have the sandal-wearing weirdo removed from the premises. But looking at the situation from a Jewish culture standpoint, it made perfect sense for those young men to take off with Jesus.

From birth, the goal of a Jewish boy was to be a rabbi. Over the course of many years, the boys would be weeded out based on their abilities to memorize and understand scripture. So eventually the number of boys set to become rabbis was very small. Rabbi was the most prestigious position in the Jewish community; it was every boy's dream job; it was every parent's wish for a son.

So by the time Jesus was approaching these young Jewish men, they had already been rejected. They were considered unworthy of being rabbis. But then this rabbi comes along and says, "Follow Me." Can you imagine their reactions? It would be like the unathletic, goofy kid getting a call from the Dallas Cowboys to come play running back. It would be like the girl who can't sing to save her life getting chosen as the winner of American Idol. It was preposterous. Of course they dropped what they were doing and went with no questions asked. It was the opportunity of a lifetime.

But we don't have the same reaction do we? We usually turn out to be more like the rich, young ruler who wasn't willing to give up everything to follow Jesus. We like the idea of Jesus, but we're not willing to sacrifice our comfort for his sake.

Maybe the problem is that we know how the story unfolded. I mean the disciples didn't know how it was all gonna turn out. "Follow Me" was easy. Jesus was new and interesting. What He offered was appealing on numerous levels. They would be prestigious members of society; they would be honored members of their families. They weren't aware of the exile, persecution, and death to come.

I guess since we know the consequences of following Jesus, it makes that decision harder. We've got more information to consider. Yet, Jesus doesn't really care how hard that decision is. He doesn't try to sugarcoat anything to bring more people on board.

If anyone wants to come with Me, he must deny himself, take up his cross daily, and follow Me.

-Luke 9:23

It's your choice. If you want to follow Him, then deny yourself, grab your cross, and come on. If you don't want to do that—if you don't think He's worth it—then so be it. Jesus isn't preaching some prosperity gospel where everyone gets in. He's not a motivational speaker trying to make everyone feel good. He makes it painfully clear that most won't get in but a few will. And if you want to go with Him, you have to follow Him.

I love how the disciples reacted once they had all the information. Jesus died, rose again, gave the great commission, and said "Follow Me" for the last time. But that "Follow Me" was a little more challenging. It had some serious consequences. It required a complete upheaval of comfort. It required death. For some it meant death of the physical body by martyrdom. For all of them—and for you and me—it meant death of the self. Yet, they didn't waver. They didn't stop and study what it would look like to follow Jesus. They went out and did it. And they saw first-hand what would happen to them; they saw Jesus beaten and nailed to a cross. But they didn't care. All they wanted was to be with Jesus. So they denied themselves, picked up their crosses, and followed Him.

How bad do you want to be with Jesus? On a daily basis, are you denying what *you* want, picking up your cross, and following after Him?

You can't just want to do it; you can't just study it and think about it. You have to *be* about it. Following Him has to be an active, everyday pursuit.

I assure you: There is no one who has left a house, wife or

brothers, parents or children because of the kingdom of God, who will not receive many times more at this time, and eternal life in the age to come.

-Luke 18:29-30

4. People

Our deepest fear is not that we are inadequate. Our deepest fear is that we are powerful beyond measure. It is our light, not our darkness that most frightens us. We ask ourselves, who am I to be brilliant, gorgeous, talented, fabulous? Actually, who are you not to be? You are a child of God. Your playing small does not serve the world. There is nothing enlightened about shrinking so that other people won't feel insecure around you. We are all meant to shine, as children do. We were born to make manifest the glory of God that is within us. It's not just in some of us; it's in everyone. And as we let our own light shine, we unconsciously give other people permission to do the same. As we are liberated from our own fear, our presence automatically liberates others.

-Marianne Williamson

People make the world of college go round. The relationships you make over the next four or so years will influence you for the rest of your life. And how you interact with others is the greatest proof of how you feel about God.

Whoever does not do what is right is not of God, especially the one who does not love his brother.

-1 John 3:10

As mentioned earlier, loving the people around you is the

second most important thing in life. Loving God is the only thing that should come before loving others, yet loving people shows a genuine love for God.

In college, you're going to come in contact with an insane amount of people from all walks of life. And as a Christian, you have a certain responsibility to all of them.

Professors

You're going to deal with professors daily. Some are Christians. Most aren't. There will be a few that you'll really cling to and who will genuinely want to help you. There will be a lot that don't care about you at all. Get over it. It's ok if not everybody likes you. The biggest thing is to not make any assumptions about the people teaching your classes. Trust me when I tell you these people are complicated, intelligent, and experienced. And they might just surprise you.

A friend of mine took a lower level religion class during his freshman year, and the professor was an absolute jerk. During every class he presented a different way to disprove God. He criticized the Bible. And he picked on the Christian students in the room. This guy had a real knack for getting under my friend's skin, and they would often get into heated debates. The professor had years of experience and would often make my friend and the other Christians in the class look foolish. It was definitely not one of my friend's favorite classes.

About a year later my friend found himself taking the same professor in a regular history class. But to my friend's surprise, the guy was a completely different person. He was almost pleasant. Come to find out, he didn't believe any of the stuff he was saying in the religion class. He was just bored and got a kick out of Christians getting riled up. He was actually a decent human being who just wanted people to think more critically about their faith.

My point is that you never know what you're gonna get.

Professors are complex people. Be patient with them. When they question or mock your faith, answer them to the best of your ability.

But do this with gentleness and respect, keeping a clear conscience, so that those who speak maliciously against your good behavior in Christ may be ashamed of their slander.

-1 Peter 3:16

Avoid heated discussions. Nothing good comes from them. If you want to argue back and forth trying to prove God, have fun. I personally checked out of that debate a long time ago. I realized that a debate isn't going to change anything, especially with a professor. These discussions are for your head; God works through your heart.

You have to understand that professors have years of experience and training on how to argue. You're not even in the same weight class with them. Plus, getting upset and squabbling with a teacher isn't exactly going to help your case. So if you have something to say, be respectful and speak with calmness. You know the saying, "you have to give respect to get respect;" well, that's not the case here. It doesn't matter if your professor is seriously disrespecting you or your faith; no matter what, you treat her with respect and take the utmost care with what you say in response. Your professor should see the greatness of Jesus by how you react to her criticism.

Don't buy in to the cliché that all professors are Christian hating atheists. It's just not the case at all. My senior year I had a chemistry teacher who stood in front of a class of two hundred and held up a chart showing the processes of metabolic proteins and said, "Looking at this, I don't see how anyone could believe we weren't created by a higher being." I was a little taken aback. I wasn't exactly expecting a chemist to say something like that.

Here was a guy at the top of his field in a profession that is notorious for not believing in a god, and he was telling this room full of people that one must exist. It was awesome. I talked to him after class and he explained to me that he had literally seen things through a microscope that no one else on the planet had ever witnessed before, and the sheer complexity of it all pointed to a divine creation.

He tore the professor stereotype to pieces. And you just might find one or two that do the same. Hopefully, you won't be as surprised as I was.

Non-Christians

College has become a fairly hostile environment for Christianity. Unless you're attending a Christian school, you'll probably be in the minority when it comes to faith. Some view this as discouraging. I see it as an awesome opportunity. God is giving you the chance to influence people on a daily basis, and whether you like it or not, how you react to these opportunities is a big deal.

Talking to non-Christians about Jesus is a pretty difficult thing to do for most of us. There are some folks who are naturals and have no trouble sharing their faith, but the rest of us would rather jump off a bridge. It's understandable. Opening up about your faith leaves you wide open for rejection and ridicule which is tough for most people to handle. However, from what I've seen and experienced, the main reason we don't like to do it is because we're really bad at it.

I'm a huge football fan. I love the NFL, and Super Bowl Sunday is a day of reverence for me. One Super Sunday when I was living in the dorm, I came downstairs to the lobby around eight A.M. to set up a spot directly in front of the big screen. I was looking forward to the next fifteen or so hours of football coverage, but I noticed a group of Christ Ambassadors on the other side of the room having a small prayer service. So, I waited until they finished to turn the TV on. When they got done, I took my seat on the couch, and I launched into football paradise. A few minutes later, a girl sat down across from me. I had never seen her before, but she was cute, and when she started talking about football, I became instantly attracted to her. She asked me all sorts of questions about the game and who I thought was going to win and why. She told me her own predictions, and we had a nice ten minute conversation. But then, it happened. She asked, "So, do you know Jesus?"

I felt betrayed. What I thought was a conversation between two football fans was actually an attempt to convert me. She wasn't flirting with me because she thought I was attractive; she just wanted to sell me some fire insurance. Our entire interaction was a lie. I immediately became skeptical of everything she said. And as soon as I told her I was a Christian with a good relationship with Jesus, she got up and left. On to the next one I guess.

The church will often get caught up in the numbers game. We become glorified salespeople trying to push a product. But Jesus is not a commodity, and he never intended for us to peddle "get out of hell" free cards.

You have to check your agenda at the door. Never go into a conversation or get involved with a relationship with conversion as the main goal. People see right through that. They may see what you're doing right off the bat, or like my situation, they might figure it out when you abruptly change the topic. Whatever the case, people don't appreciate used car salesmen, and they won't appreciate you acting like one.

If you know a guy who desperately needs Christ, go love on him. Be his friend. Do everything you can to help him. If you meet a girl struggling with a tough situation, go love on her. Be a shoulder to cry on. Let her know someone cares.

No agendas—just good old fashioned love.

So neither he who plants nor he who waters is anything, but only God, who makes things grow. The man who plants and the man who waters have one purpose, and each will be rewarded according to his own labor.

-1 Corinthians 3:7-8

Used car salesmen act the way they do because they work off commission. The more they sell, the more they make. If they can talk you into upgrading to a six disc CD changer and an extended warranty, they make more money. But the kingdom of God is not a used car lot. It's not up to us to "make a sale;" it's up to God. He simply puts us in positions to plant and water seeds. By loving people without an agenda, you're planting seeds. By developing deeper relationships with people, you're watering those seeds. But God is the reason those seeds grow. That takes a lot of pressure off you and me. It's not up to us to get people to buy Jesus. We're here to show them what a life with Jesus looks like. Basically, we work in the marketing department.

I've heard it said that God is a good guy with bad PR. I've found that to be pretty true. A lot of Christians are trying to sell something they don't even live out. (I wonder if that's gonna work.) Here's the deal: don't get caught up in the numbers game; don't try to push Jesus as a product. Instead, demonstrate what it means to be a Christian on an everyday basis. That's how you bring people to know Jesus. You don't tell them how to get there; you show them the way.

I'm not really one to toss around Jesus and Bible verses in everyday conversation. It works for some people, but it's just not my style. I take a more subtle approach when talking to non-Christians. I talk to them about sports. I ask questions about class schedules and which professors are good. I get to know them as friends. I'll invite a guy to a party before I'll invite him to church. Why? Because people aren't going to listen to you unless they sense you like them. On the surface, it looks like Jesus interacted with people in passing. It appears that He met them, changed their lives, and left. But if you really think about it, that's not what He did at all. Jesus already knew every single person He came into contact with. He knew their struggles, their sins, their pains, and their faith. He already had intimate knowledge of their entire life stories. And with that knowledge, He brought them out of darkness. Take the woman at the well for instance (John 4). Jesus wasn't talking as a stranger. It wasn't a cold call, so to speak. He knew who she was and how she lived. The same should go for us. We obviously don't know people before they were in the womb like God does, so we have to work a little harder to get to know someone. But it's through that knowledge and bond of relationship that we can truly change people's lives.

What happens in a person's soul is between him and God. All I can do is love him and plant seeds. I can encourage him and pray for opportunities to share Christ. You can't force Jesus on people in the same way you can't force someone to quit an addiction. They have to want to. So many people are addicted to the world. It's up to us to show them that there's something better.

Are you living a life that others want? What does your lifestyle say about your faith? Do you realize who's watching?

Once you get to know someone, don't force the issue. Conversations about Jesus will often get really awkward because we try to impose them instead of allowing them to happen naturally. Pray for the chance to talk about Christ, and then make good on it when it pops up. Just remember:

[D]o not worry about what to say or how to say it. At that time you will be given what to say, for it will not be you speaking, but the Spirit of your Father speaking through you.

-Matthew 10:19-20

It's when you realize how little you have to do with someone coming to know God that you become the most effective. Thinking you're the main reason a person accepts Christ takes the glory away from Him and means you're more concerned about stroking your ego than loving your friend. So just let go. Don't worry about what to say. Let God speak through you. And when He does, don't take the credit for yourself.

At the same time, you have to realize that not everyone is going to see God as you do.

For the message of the cross is foolishness to those who are perishing, but to us who are being saved it is the power of God.

-1 Corinthians 1:18

Everyone gets to choose. Some will realize the awesome power of God. Some won't. That's life. Each person will have to stand before God and answer for that choice. And when people reject your faith, all you can do is continue to love them and pray that God turns their hearts. Don't give up hope, but understand that you can't *make* someone a follower of Christ. Either he'll choose God or he won't. You just have to keep planting and watering seeds.

Christians

This is how we have come to know love: He laid down His life for us. We should also lay down our lives for our brothers.

-1 John 3:16

Do you remember in Genesis when Cain told God, "I'm not my brother's keeper" after killing Abel? It's interesting how that line became so popular. I've heard it used a ton of times, and since it's from the Bible, it must be true, right?

Wrong.

You *are* your brother's keeper.

As Christians, we are responsible for the well-being of the people around us, especially other Christians. Just as Jesus gave his life for us, we should give our lives for others. That doesn't necessarily mean your heart has to stop beating. It could just as easily mean the sacrificing of your time, energy, or money. Whatever the case, we have an obligation to other Christians.

How is the world supposed to believe in God when His people don't even take care of their own? Hopefully, you're going to be around a lot of Christians while off at school, and that means you're going to have a lot of chances to love and help other men and women of God. Make good on those opportunities.

If a guy needs a ride, go pick him up. If a girl has the flu, carry her some soup. It's not hard. It just takes putting yourself second. It takes laying down what you want and helping someone else.

As Christians, we have to come together. Christianity is not about solo efforts. It's a team game. When one wins, we all win. When one loses, we all lose. We have to get away from individualism. When one part of the body is struggling, we have to rally around that part to get it going again. If you see a Christian in need and don't help, I really have to question whether you're really all in. We're talking about family here. If you can't help the people in your own family, how do you plan to help anybody else? How can we bring hope to the lost if we can't even bring it to each other?

The world will know we are Christians by our love. I know you've heard that before. But that love starts in-house.

Finding a New Group

One of the biggest challenges of going off to school is finding a new group. Meeting new people can be awkward, but getting connected with a Christian group on campus is one of the most essential things to do once you arrive.

Shop around. Just because you grew up in a Baptist church doesn't mean you should be a member of the Baptist Campus Ministry. Just because you grew up a Methodist doesn't mean you'll have the best experience at the Wesley Foundation. Visit all of them. Get to know the people at each one. Then make an informed decision. The affiliation is not that important. Where you fit in is what matters. If you don't fit in with the people and leaders, you're not likely to keep coming. So find a place that feels comfortable.

Also, don't get connected to the gatherings or events. Connect to the people. It's nice if you like the worship music they play or the sermons that get preached, but it's far more important and valuable to get involved with the members of the group. A service rarely changes people. Experiences and relationships almost always do.

During my junior year, I went to a service on campus on Thursday nights. The guy that led worship was phenomenal, and he was the main reason I kept coming back. So when he transferred to another school, I stopped going.

I wasn't connected to the people. I was there for the music. And when the music changed, there was nothing keeping me there anymore. So instead of worshiping God on Thursday nights, I did my own thing. Now, this wasn't one of those situations where I stopped going to church and started getting wasted and having sex instead. My lifestyle didn't really change because my lack of attendance. It just made my Thursday nights a lot less valuable. Instead of worshiping God, I would watch a movie or go out to eat. I did a ton of frivolous things while I could have been having meaningful conversations and finding more ways to love.

And I think that's where the Devil can really get us. I wasn't doing anything wrong. My Thursday nights didn't become chock-full of sin. But I wasn't doing anything of meaning either. The night just became forgettable.

Don't let your time in college be forgettable. Get involved with a group and get connected with other Christians. There's always a ton of stuff to do around campus, but most of them have little value. However, engaging in other people's lives is one of the most meaningful things you can do. So surround yourself with people of passion. Get to know them inside and out. And let them get to know you.

The original church would meet together to do a lot more than worship and learn about God. The early Christians had such a hard time with persecution, rejection, and living in a hostile environment that they needed that time together to build each other back up. Your Christian group should do the same. College is a rigorous atmosphere; you need to be around other Christians experiencing it the same way you are. If you're struggling with a certain aspect of your faith, it's important to talk to people who are dealing with the same things. When a professor starts messing with what you believe, you need people around you who have already conquered the same class. This group can really help strengthen your faith.

It's equally important to have people who will hold you accountable for your actions. Find a few friends of the same gender and meet together once a week. The phrase "accountability partner" is a little overused but you need people who care about what direction your life is going in. It's also nice to have people you can vent frustrations and difficulties to. You'll be amazed at how much better you feel afterward.

A Christian organization will also provide you with opportunities to serve. Most groups organize mission trips and sponsor campus events throughout the year. And if you want to really get involved, take on a leadership role. If you see a need, volunteer to help fill it.

I can't forget about the food. Christian organizations are known for providing delicious, home-cooked food. Just get there early; it runs out fast. (These groups are also a good place to find teammates for intramurals.)

Shine

He used to say soulshine,

It's better than sunshine,

It's better than moonshine,

Damn sure better than the rain.

Hey now people don't mind,

We all get this way sometime,

Got to let your soul shine, shine till the break of day.

-The Allman Brothers Band

It's often said that teenagers today "just don't know how good they've got it." "Back in my day, to get to school, we had to walk fifteen miles in the snow, uphill both ways, with no feet." You might not have heard *that* specifically but probably something close. And in a lot of ways, you have had it a lot easier. Yet, there is one major difference that makes living in this generation exponentially more difficult: the Internet.

Now, every embarrassing thing you say or do can be immediately captured and uploaded to the web for the world to see. Any idiot with a camera phone can document your awkward moments and plaster them on Facebook. Any half-wit with an internet connection can put your mistake up on Youtube, and fifteen million views later, you're the most famous person you know, but it's not because you worked hard or came up with some awesome, new idea. It's because you threw up all over yourself at a party.

What a lot of people don't understand is that once it's on the web, it's on there forever. No matter what you do, the picture or video will be saved on a server until the end of time. But you deleted all those embarrassing pictures from Facebook? They still exist. Facebook still has them saved. And Facebook can even sell that content if it wants. (If you don't believe me, check the Terms and Conditions you agreed to when you set up your account.) In other words, at no other point in history have people had to be more aware of their actions at all times. Old folks don't know how good they had it. Back in their day, telephones were only used to make phone calls. Embarrassing moments only lived in memories which would eventually degrade and be lost forever. What a bunch of lightweights.

But if you look at this from a Christian standpoint, it might actually be a good thing. At no other point in history has it been so easy to find out who a person is without having to actually talk to them. Thanks to the internet, you can now be a positive influence on people you've never even met. It's possible to let your light shine to millions without having to leave your desk. I'm not saying you have to fill up your "about" page with Jesus and Bible verses, but keep in mind that the online profile is now one of the main ways people get to know each other. This is why the internet is also like a challenge from the Devil himself. He's just waiting to show you as a phony, and when you think no one is watching and you let your guard down, he'll send pictures of it to everyone you know.

Let your light shine before men, so that they may see your good works and give glory to your Father in heaven.

-Matthew 5:16

Do you see the greatness in this verse? You don't do good works to get right with God; good deeds won't get you into heaven. Instead, you let your light shine so that other people will give glory to God. You don't pursue excellence to become famous or feel good about yourself; you pursue it so that others will come to know Jesus.

Over the next few years, you're gonna be around so many people it's not even funny. And most of them won't know Jesus. Your roommate probably won't be a Christian. Your professors will be skeptical of God. Your classmates will be apathetic towards your thoughts on faith. Basically, you're going to be surrounded by people who need Christ to impact their lives. In other words, you have an incredible opportunity to let your light shine.

Christians don't exactly have the best reputation on college campuses. In the same way a handful of terrorists have caused Muslims to be stereotyped and discriminated against, a small group of idiots calling themselves Christians have tried to ruin things for the rest of us. When people find out you're a Christian, they're liable to have thoughts of the people who protest funerals of homosexuals and blow up abortion clinics. Their initial ideas might be that you're an intolerant, close-minded simpleton who believes in a bunch of silly myths. It's not a bad thing for them to think this before they get to know you. However, it's a terrible thing if it's what they think after seeing who you really are. When people hear the word "Christian," all sorts of images will go through their heads. It's up to you to prove those images right or wrong.

Letting your light shine and showing people what it means to be a Christ follower will leave lasting impressions. It should be your goal everyday to blow people away with your forgiveness, compassion, and love. When others see you, they should see Jesus. They should get a glimpse of what it means to have a relationship with God.

If a friend screws you over, forgive him. If a classmate thinks

Jesus is a hoax, respect her ideas. If a professor bullies you, say nice things about him. If a girl hates you, pray for her. If you know a guy who is gay, love him. I'm not saying you should condone how people live their lives, but you should love them in spite of all transgressions. Why? Because God loves you in spite of yours, and loving people the way Christ does is the only thing that will truly change the world. Light up the darkness.

Live in a way that people will want what you have. And when they ask you about it, don't take the credit for yourself. Give all the glory to God. Make it clear that without Him nothing in your life would be possible. Everything in your life should point to Him. No matter where you are or what you're doing—whether you're in class, at a football game, in the dorm, or on Facebook—your light should be shining all the while.

I've got a friend named Liz who got married a while back. Things were going great until Liz found out her husband, Jake, was cheating on her. They split up and were working through the process of divorce when Liz started getting e-mails from Jake's mistress, Amy. Now, Amy had a knack for typing up malicious e-mails, and she made sure Liz knew just how long Jake had been cheating on her, how many times, and where. Amy sent messages claiming she and Jake were going to get married as soon as the divorce papers were finalized and reported all the cruel things Jake had said about Liz. Amy even sent one message that stated Jake was now with her because she could actually have a baby. (Liz had had a miscarriage a few months prior.) It was some truly awful stuff.

After the divorce, Amy and Jake got married, and Liz didn't hear from them for a good long while. (Which she was definitely fine with.) Over a year later, an interesting e-mail showed up in Liz's inbox from Amy. Apparently, Jake had cheated on her too, and she needed advice on how to proceed with a divorce. It seemed that Liz found herself an opportunity for revenge that most people only dream about. But she didn't take it. She forgave Amy for all the despicable things that had been said and advised her on the next steps to take against Jake. Liz had an incredible chance to get back at someone who had caused her a great deal of pain, but instead she chose to lend a hand. Would you have done the same? You will only get a handful of moments like that in life—moments to shine with Christ like love and forgiveness. But how will you react? I hope it's in such a way that gives glory to God.

Push Pull

Confidence is contagious. So is lack of Confidence.

-Vince Lombardi

People in general are scared. They're nervous. They're insecure. They think about and *want* to do a lot of things but very rarely get bold enough to take the first step. Now, there a lot of people out there that prefer the "push" method to get others to live more boldly. Tons of motivational speakers, preachers, writers, and youth leaders do their best to push others to go confidently toward the life they're capable of—the life that God yearns for them to have. But a technique that works infinitely better—a way that can create revolutionary change—is the "pull" method.

To push someone requires you to be behind them, and well, you don't lead very effectively from the back. To pull someone is the ultimate tool of leadership. And I'm not talking about grabbing someone by the arm and yanking them forward. That's merely a glorified push. I'm referring to the natural, subconscious, inherent, magnetic pull humans have to one another.

When I was in high school a group of friends and I were hanging out at the lake. Four of us decided we wanted to go jump off Chimney Rock. Now, where I come from, that's no small feat. I mean people have died doing that. We're talking about a giant cliff around a hundred feet from the water that comes with devastating consequences if you make a mistake. It's hard to climb up to. And it's even harder to look down from. As a group of idiots, we decided it must be done.

We scaled the cliff to the top, and looking down, we discovered it was much higher than any of us had previously thought. So we stared at each other. The boats down below looked like toys in a bathtub. We tried to decide who would jump first. After a long debate that resolved nothing, we went silent. Without warning, the guy next to me took off running and leapt. The rest of us watched as he got smaller and smaller. Splash. After what seemed like a long time, he came to the surface. Alive. Now, I had to jump. So I did.

No one pushed me to hurl myself off that cliff. But a friend showed me it was possible. Him proving it could be done pulled me over the edge. Now, this is a minor, somewhat moronic, event in my life, but the natural pull people have can cause radical changes.

I'm a big fan of Rosa Parks. What I love about her is that she had no idea what her one act of defiance would cause. She didn't refuse to move because of some pre-arranged plan; she wasn't part of an elaborate scheme. She was just tired. Her feet hurt. So she sat down. And that one bold move reverberated throughout the entire country. It was the match that set fire to a movement that changed everything. It proves that one choice can pull a nation of people together. You can push and prod people all you want, but until some brave soul steps up to pull others forward, change will not occur.

At the time I was arrested I had no idea it would turn into this. It was just a day like any other day. The only thing that made it significant was that the masses of the people joined in.

-Rosa Parks

Gabe Barrett

People are waiting to be pulled toward the lives they're capable of. They just need someone to show them the way. As Jesus has shown us, we must show others.

For a long time religion was a push. It was all rules, laws, and regulations. Rabbis and priests told people how to live, and every now and then a prophet would come along and offer new insight into the heart of God. But then Jesus came. God decided to stop pushing and start pulling us to Him. He showed us how to live, how to interact with people, and how to be holy. He showed us how to love. He came to draw us nearer to Him and to empower His followers to spread light into darkness. Jesus was the pull that conquered the world. He came so that we might come after Him. Now it's up to us to continue His pull. Pushing people to Christ is usually ineffective. It's one thing to tell a girl Jesus loves her; it's an entirely different thing to show her.

Does your life pull people toward Jesus? Or do you spend your time trying to push people to God? Have you even thought about how your actions lead others to or away from Christ?

5. Physical

Do you not know that your body is a temple of the Holy Spirit, who is in you, whom you have received from God? You are not your own; you were bought at a price. Therefore honor God with your body.

-1 Corinthians 6:19-20

Treating the body as a temple is one of the hardest things for a Christian college student to do. And no wonder. College presents temptation on a silver platter, and we often have a hard time saying no; and it doesn't take long for the temple of God to become ruins. If you want to conquer college, you have to conquer your body. You have to kick temptation in the stomach, and punch the Devil in the face. You're going to have to get over pleasing yourself. And it's tough. Believe me, I understand how tough it is. But I want you to know it's possible. All it takes is faith, self-discipline, and making smart decisions.

Your Body

A lazy person is as bad as someone who destroys things.

-Proverbs 18:9

Don't get lazy just because you're off at school. I've seen so many people come in freshman year in great health and leave a year later in terrible condition. And it's all because they got lazy with eating and exercise.

The biggest thing you have to understand is that your body is not your own. As Paul says, "you were bought at a price." Jesus paid dearly for us, and our bodies are gifts straight from Him. So how you treat your body reflects how you feel about God. In other words, becoming lazy and "letting yourself go" shows how much you really appreciate God's gift to you.

You only get one body. So what you put into it and do with it matter. Drinking a gallon of soda and eating pizza everyday probably aren't the best ways to take care of yourself. Avoiding physical activity in favor of video games won't get you very far either. I'm not saying you have to be a gym rat and only drink water during fifty calorie meals, but it is vital that you become conscious of what's going in your body and how often you exercise.

Now, this isn't necessarily about gaining a bunch of weight. Everybody gains weight in college[4]. This isn't about God loving you any more or less based on your waistline. Succumbing to the freshman fifteen doesn't make you a bad Christian. The issue is how you treat what is on loan from God. Do you destroy it? Or do you keep it in fine working condition?

Here's the deal: the more out of shape you are and the more you consistently put garbage into your system and refuse to work it off, the more likely you are to become sick, injured, or unproductive.

Never be lazy, but work hard and serve the Lord enthusiastically.

-Romans 12:11

It's much harder to go out and serve God when you're laid up in the bed sick. It's hard to shine like a city on a hill when you've got dark circles under your eyes. It's hard to make a stand for Christ when you broke your ankle due to calcium deficiency. Allowing your body to get in a defunct state won't automatically make your life fruitless; it'll just give you more obstacles to overcome. Why make it harder on yourself when you don't have to? Prevention is always easier than finding a cure. All it takes is making smart choices and a little hard work. So don't wait until tomorrow to start eating right. Don't wait around for New Year's to start a fitness program. Don't be lazy. Treat your body like it's a gift from God.

At the same time, don't turn training into an idol. I've known a couple guys who went to church in the weight room where the barbell was their Jesus and the squat rack was their Holy Ghost. They worshipped their biceps and prayed to the treadmill. Don't fall into the trap of vanity. I'm not saying you shouldn't be proud of how your had work pays off, but don't make your fitness into a selfish ordeal. It's not about exercising your ego. It's about keeping your body in the most optimal working condition so you can better serve and glorify God.

That brings me to modesty. A Christian who lacks modesty has a self-esteem issue. A person must have trouble with self-esteem if being acknowledged and recognized by God isn't enough, so he or she has to show off to others. Whether it's a plunging neckline or a skintight muscle shirt, they want to be noticed and validated based on their appearance.

Is it wrong for a guy to take his shirt off or for a girl to wear a tight dress? No. The sinful nature comes about with *why* a guy takes his shirt off and *why* a girl wears a tight dress. And if the reason is to impress others, there's a problem. In America, we worship beautiful people. However, God sees through what will shortly fade away and peers into a person's heart. He doesn't care what the outside looks like; He isn't impressed by cleavage or abs. God is impressed by humility. So the question is what's more important: to impress other people or to impress God? Once again, you shouldn't just let yourself go, but you should pay attention to *why* you're wearing a certain article of clothing or not wearing it for that matter.

[L]et us purify ourselves from everything that contaminates body and spirit, perfecting holiness out of reverence for God.

-2 Corinthians 7:1

Food is an important aspect of college. After tuition, it's where most of your money will go. And while I realize how convenient and cheap the dollar menu is, it's important to limit how much rubbish goes into your stomach. I'm not saying you have to go buy all organic food and cook every meal yourself, but you should pay attention to what goes in your body. Crappy food makes you feel crappy. Fast food does nothing to help you remember what you studied, and it's definitely not gonna make you better at intramurals. Plus, eating and drinking enough garbage has consequences that will last for the rest of your life. I've got a friend who drank so many sodas and energy drinks that the acid eroded the lining in his stomach. Now he has a hard time eating or drinking anything, and it's not exactly a problem that magically goes away. Another friend is so addicted to caffeine that he goes into withdrawal after a few days without having it. He gets bad headaches that only go away when he drinks a large soda.

Now, I know fast food is sometimes the only option, and I understand that an energy drink can provide a nice pick-me-up. And I realize they're not going to harm you if you don't overdo it. It's all about portion size. You need to limit the contaminates that go into your body. If you always had someone cook for you growing up, college might be a tough transition. You're gonna have to pay extra attention to what and how much goes in your system. Most campuses have all-you-can-eat buffets, but don't take that as a challenge to eat until your pants get tight. And drink some dang water. Don't fill up your cup with empty calories and sugar. Drink something that will help you live better and think better. High fructose corn syrup will do neither. And if you can't do it for yourself, do it out of reverence for God. At least have some respect for the One who created the body you're living in, and stop putting junk into it.

Basically what I'm asking is this: How can you expect to have victory over the world when you can't even conquer the cafeteria? If you don't even have enough self-discipline to control portion sizes, how are you gonna control the stronger human desires?

It's important to get a handle on food and exercise. They're part of the foundation for serving God and avoiding sin. Crappy food and laziness make you tired. And fatigue makes cowards of us all[5]. Being worn-out makes it harder to go out and love other people, and fending off Satan is much tougher when you're exhausted. So do yourself a favor by eating right and exercising. Not only will it show gratitude and respect for what God has created and given you, but it will also help keep you physically, mentally, and spiritually strong.

Partying

I'm not much of a "partier," but I love going to parties. I don't really care about drinking, but I have a great time watching drunk people make fools of themselves. I don't see the point in going crazy and acting like an idiot, but it's extremely entertaining to observe people who don't share that sentiment. Some Christian authors would warn you away from parties. I personally don't see much harm in them. Go have fun; just stay in control. If the party starts getting tense or out of hand, go home. **When in doubt, get out**. It's that simple.

Jesus had a little partying spirit in Him. He was constantly going over to other people's houses and having a good time. His first miracle happened at a party and involved alcohol no less. I think it's safe to say Jesus was a fan of the social gathering. But you'll notice that He always stayed in control. He never got belligerent and told the Pharisees where to go. He remained quite sober while telling them.

Do not get drunk on wine, which leads to debauchery[6]. Instead, be filled with the Spirit.

-Ephesians 5:18

First of all, if you're underage, alcohol is out of the question. It's illegal, so don't drink it. That's about as simple as it gets. However, if you've reached the ripe age of twenty-one, then feel free to enjoy it in moderation. I personally think it's a waste of money, and I've never found it to add anything of value to an experience. But if it's your thing, go for it. Just realize that alcohol often leads to making poor choices that you wouldn't have made while sober. Nice Christian girls get pregnant all the time and peaceful Christian guys go to jail regularly thanks to a little booze. Alcohol can lead to things much worse than a hangover. Don't take it lightly; it'll burn you.

For the record, if alcohol becomes a requirement for you to have fun or if you "need" it, then you're on the path to addiction and you should seek help. Seriously. Drinking should not be the reason you enjoy yourself. And the deeper you get in, the harder it is to get out. This is not a game, and alcohol is not something to play with. Lives get ruined on a daily basis thanks to it. Don't become a statistic.

I've known people to attend parties with a missionary mindset. They see the frat house as a faraway land full of non-believers waiting to give their lives to Jesus. But let's just be honest here; sharing Christ with a person who won't remember what happened when he wakes up is kind of fruitless. You're not going to bring a drunk person to Jesus. Any commitment made while intoxicated is pretty much void. So instead of going to a party trying to save everyone, just go have fun and show others what it looks like for a Christian to hang out at a party. Do what Jesus did. Listen to people. Get to know them. Show them that Christians aren't all uptight, self-righteous snobs. Some of the best conversations I've ever had happened at parties. Alcohol gets people to talk more than they normally would which has led to some amazing discussions about God. And the most interesting thing is that when you respect what others have to say, they actually listen to your ideas on the subject. Wow. Who would have thought?

A very good friend of mine is agnostic. During numerous parties, he and I would sit outside away from the music and discuss evolution, morals, and anything else that came to mind. He would lay out his beliefs; I would lay out mine. After the party, I would either drive him home or he would sleep on my couch. No matter what was said or what he believed, there wasn't any doubt in his mind that I cared about him. To this day, the offer stands that if he ever needs a couch to sleep on, mine is available.

That's why you go to parties. Sure, having fun is part of it, but it's so much more important to get to know people. A party is a great time to let loose, but it's a better time to show people love. Be a designated driver[7]. Interact with people in kindness. Be a peacekeeper. Whether you like it or not, as a Christian, you have a responsibility to the people around you. Make good on that responsibility.

And just so I know that I covered it: stay away from drugs. I mean, really? Drugs? Really? Does anyone even have to tell you that at this point? They're illegal. They destroy your body. They erode your mind. They lead to life-altering decisions. I could keep going, but you've heard it all before. Drugs are easy to get a hold of in college. Everybody knows a guy who knows a guy who can score what you need. But come on. You're better than that.

Drugs are marvelous if you want to escape, but reality is so rich, why escape?

-Geraldine Chaplin

Dating

So, originally, I was just gonna bullcrap my way through this section and steer clear of all the skeletons in my closet. However, the more I tried that, the more I got writer's block. So, I figure God wants me to actually use those experiences to shed some light on a heavily debated subject.

With that said, I was such an idiot about relationships in college. You'll be an idiot about them too if you're not careful. Most people turn dating into a game. It's one team versus another, winner take all. But the more I played the game, the more I saw how ridiculous the entire thing was, and the more I realized the person I had become. I had gotten really good at the game, but all I won was emptiness.

Dating is not a game. The stakes are too high to label it such. We're dealing with hearts and emotions here. If you break a bone, it heals in a few weeks; if you break a heart, it might never fully recover. It's important to understand that. I didn't get it for a long time, and I left a path of destruction because of it. I was quick to get into relationships and quick to get out of them. And I'll have to answer to God one day for the damage I caused.

Patience is probably the most important aspect of dating. It sucks sometimes and can be annoyingly frustrating, but in the end it will keep you and others from a ton of heartache.

My advice to any freshman is to wait at least a semester before getting in to anything serious. Thank goodness, this is one of the few things I got right. I transferred to a different school during that first Christmas break, and a committed relationship would have probably stopped me from doing that. So once you arrive on campus, get settled in before you start looking for love. You've got enough to worry about. A boyfriend or girlfriend will only make your life more cluttered.

That first semester is pivotal in finding a new group of friends, and the responsibilities associated with a significant other will greatly hamper you meeting new people to hang out with. Plus, three months later when you break up, you'll have no significant other and no friends. If the relationship is meant to be, it can wait until at least second semester.

Before you get into anything serious, how's your relationship with God? Are you praying? Are you involved in a church or campus organization? Are you studying the Bible regularly? Are you truly seeking Him on a daily basis? If you're not doing those things, your relationships will probably be doomed from the start. Seek God first. Get your relationship with Him right before venturing into a dating relationship. You don't have to be some perfect Christian or anything, but your focus should be God. You should be fitting dating into His will not the other way around.

For a while, I was just going through the motions. I read my Bible and went to worship services. I knew I loved God and I knew He loved me, but I wasn't *in love* with Him. I wasn't actively pursuing Him with my life. And the relationships I wound up in reflected that. They were about me and what I wanted. They had nothing to do with what God wanted. Looking back, there were a couple times when He saved me from myself and kept me from making some extraordinarily foolish decisions, but it wasn't until much later that I realized how far off the right path I had gone. So, be patient. Chase after God and let Him bring someone to you in *His* time. It might suck for a while, but it's better than getting into a bunch of unhealthy relationships because you're too selfish to give it over to God. Trust me.

Let's get into the *point* of dating a little more. The reason you date someone is to see if you want to marry him or her. Casual dating is both a waste of money and a waste of time. Think of it as a long interview process. Don't worry, the other person is interviewing you too. But before you get that far, it's important to have some criteria for the kind of person you want to end up with. It may sound silly, but it's a good idea to write out all the character and personality traits that are important to you. I realize how cold and calculating this sounds and how much it lacks in emotion, but it's vital groundwork for establishing a healthy, lasting relationship. My list looks something like this:

What's Important to Me

-follows Jesus

-can tell a good story

-funny but also knows when to be serious

-pretty

-motivated

-doesn't depend on me for happiness

-interacts well with my friends

You get the idea. It's okay to have really high standards, and it's okay to not date someone because he or she doesn't meet your criteria. My problem was that I waited way too long to make a list. Instead of getting to know a girl and seeing if she fit into what I was looking for, I just rushed into a relationship with her. So when I found out she couldn't tell a good story or didn't enjoy being around my friends or couldn't solve simple math equations, I ended the relationship and came off looking like a jerk. But more than that, I caused her emotional damage. There's no excuse for that. And if I had established ahead of time what I wanted in a partner and had gotten to know girls slowly, most all of those relationships would have never happened and that damage would have been prevented.

If the other person isn't a Christian, why would you consider dating? I fell into that trap too. And I wasn't even thinking of it as missionary dating which is a truly ridiculous idea by the way. I realize there are some success stories out there of a Christian bringing a non-Christian to Jesus in a dating relationship, but it's kind of like the lottery. Yeah, someone has to win it, but there are a ton more people who just threw their money away. It's a lot more likely that your non-Christian partner will bring you down.

Anyway, I thought this girl was really hot, and I was selfish, so I got into a relationship with her even though she wasn't a Christian. Needless to say, it was not a healthy ordeal. She had a real way of bringing out the worst in me, and I was going through a really tough time in life in general anyway, and putting both of those together didn't exactly make me the man God wanted me to be. I managed to get out of that relationship without too much harm done, but I should have never been in it in the first place.

Do not be yoked together with unbelievers. For what do righteousness and wickedness have in common? Or what fellowship can light have with darkness?

-2 Corinthians 6:14

I realize not all non-Christians are evil heathens, but the point is to not get involved in a committed relationship with someone who doesn't share your faith. It's spiritually unhealthy and creates division and strife in the relationship. It's just not worth it, no matter how hot he or she is.

After that relationship, I immediately got involved with the most Christian girl I knew. I had jumped from one end of the spectrum to the other. But the relationship was doomed from the beginning. Not because of her. She is a phenomenal human being who is changing the world for the better on a daily basis. But I was no good for anybody, and my relationship with God sucked. That relationship never had a chance, and she deserved so much better than what I had to offer.

Are you seeing the pattern in all this? Do you see how seeking selfish desires instead of God leads to ruin? Do you understand how a lack of patience causes nothing but grief? Can you sense how badly I want you to avoid the mistakes I made?

Once I finally got all my crap together—once I started being patient—God blessed me with a healthy relationship. And you would not believe how slowly I took that one. After making so many mistakes, I wanted to make sure I didn't screw it up. My relationship with God was as strong as it had ever been. I was pursuing His will for my life, and I understood what He wanted out of me. And wouldn't you know it, I ended up marrying that girl. It's funny how when you do things the right way, they work out how they're supposed to. Now, I'm not saying every healthy, God-seeking relationship is going to end in marriage. There are plenty of relationships that just aren't meant to be. But you stand a much better chance at success when you keep God first and stay patient.

I hope you'll listen to me about this stuff. I realize there's a pretty good chance you won't. Most college students prefer to do things on their own, and I get that. But do yourself a favor and avoid the mistakes I made. Your conscience will be clearer, and you'll sleep a lot better. What I'm saying is **be the model, not the warning**.

Sex

Sex is one of those topics that everyone thinks about, but the church doesn't always do the best job of talking about. It can be awkward and has a tendency to make people feel uncomfortable, so it often gets swept under the rug. Parents and youth directors frequently take the approach of "sex is bad; be abstinent or else." Now, I believe abstinence is definitely the way to go, but I think it's equally important to explain *why* it's the best option in detail.

Sex has three parts. Physical. Emotional. Spiritual. Like it or not, it's impossible to have sex without all three parts being involved. Sex, by its very design, connects people together in those three areas and creates a permanent bond. That's why sex is such a big deal. There's really no such thing as casual sex. You can have a casual relationship in which neither person gets too involved, but sex is always a deeply intimate experience. That's how we're wired. It doesn't matter what you want it to be. It doesn't matter if you *think* you can have no strings attached. It doesn't matter how you justify it in your brain.

Your heart is compromised each and every time you have sex with someone you're not married to. I realize how serious that sounds. And I realize how different our culture's view of the issue is. But trust me when I say that the more of yourself you give away, the less you have to give. Each time you have sex, you're giving away a part of you that will not return. That's why it's so important to wait until you're married, so you'll be able to give everything to the person who deserves it most.

For Guys

Most men, especially in college, focus solely on the physical aspect. They just want to screw someone. A guy meets a girl at a party and desires nothing more than to take her home and have his way with her. Or he seduces a well-known cheerleader because she would make an interesting story to tell his friends. But you have to understand that this isn't anything close to what sex is supposed to be. This kind of behavior is actually nothing more than masturbation with another person present. It's getting off to appease an animalistic instinct. It's sin at its finest.

Screwing people for the sake of screwing them is a cheap imitation for sex, but it costs the full price. Physically, it feels great. All those chemicals in your body feel good, and life couldn't be better. However, this kind of sexual contact destroys you emotionally and spiritually whether you realize it or not.

A lot of guys view sex as a validation of their manhood. The more girls they have sex with, the more of a man they are. However, this kind of behavior is not just detrimental to all parties involved but is also only carried out by selfish, little boys pretending to be men. Only a boy would treat a person as an instrument of pleasure. A full-grown man of God sees women as gifts who should be loved, respected, and fought for. Men don't view women as playthings.

How you treat a woman reveals how you feel about the One who created her. Disrespecting her is the equivalent of spitting in God's face. Using a woman for sex is no different than tearing up art painted by God, and it's something you'll have to answer for when you stand before Him.

To be a man of God, you have to be willing to lay down your life unselfishly for the woman you love. You have to be ready to fight dragons and walk through fire. Does that sound too intense? Good. Because if you're not willing to do those things, you don't deserve her. A woman of God is worth far more than any selfish pleasure.

Too many Christian guys refuse to grow up. They get Peter Pan syndrome and try to stay little boys as long as possible. Too many Christian guys are cowards. They aren't willing to fight. The good news is you get to choose. You can remain a boy and live your life as a coward only seeking women out of selfish reasons. Or you can grow up and be the man God would have you to be. It's up to you.

For Girls

Not too long ago, most women focused solely on the emotional aspect of sex. They just wanted to be loved and cared for, and they thought sex was the way to achieve the intimacy they so deeply desired. However, women are now increasingly seeking the physical aspect of sex just as men are. Yet, once again, sex under these pretenses is only a cheap imitation for the real thing. Whether a woman wants just the emotional or physical part, everything else gets thrown in too. It doesn't matter how strong you think you are; having sex with a guy you're not married to is going to cause damage. It might not show up for a while, but it's there all the same.

You are a beautiful work of art created by God. You don't need to look to sex to know your self-worth; simply look to Him. I realize what our culture tells you; I know how it pressures you to look, talk, and act. But don't buy that garbage. Don't derive your self-esteem from the world. It only leads to ruin.

At the same time, don't derive your self-esteem from guys either. Men like to conquer things; they like conquests. And a bunch of hormone driven college boys will probably try to conquer you. I'm not saying every guy is like that or that you should think everything a guy says is a lie. But be skeptical. If a guy says he loves you, ask him why. Don't assume a guy has your best interest in mind. Be patient. What do his actions tell you? And if he ever pressures you sexually, it's obvious he's only out for himself. I hope I don't have to tell you to get out of a relationship like that. Guys are a lot more manipulative than people give them credit for, and even "good" guys have been known to say whatever was necessary to get a girl to go farther than she was willing. I hope you're strong enough to put God first and avoid anyone who would have you compromise that.

It's time to become a woman of God. It's time to stop messing around with foolish little boys. If a guy isn't willing to fight for you; if he's not willing to lay down his life for you; if he's not willing to put you first; then, why would you be with him? Why would you put up with a coward? And why on earth would you have sex with him?

It's time to listen to God and not society. Our culture only wants to use you, and once it's done, it'll move on to the next one. However, God desires nothing more than to have a loving relationship with you. He just wants what's best for you. And whose approval are you seeking more: the world's or God's?

When it comes to guys, be careful, be smart, be patient. There are some really great men out there, but there are too many selfish, little boys pretending to be men for you to be hasty or carless. Don't open your life up to just anybody. Guard your heart. And get away from anyone who is careless with it. Pursue God first Let everything else stem from your relationship with Him.

A woman's heart should be so hidden in Christ, that a man should have to seek Him first to find her.

-Maya Angelou

Sex and Marriage

I'll be honest; I really wanted to find a way to make sex outside of marriage okay. I did my best to find a loophole in scripture so I could be the cool guy that said sex was alright. But you know what? It's just not there. You can take some verses out of context or twist some words to make them fit what you want, but if you read the Bible truthfully, it's obvious that sex outside of marriage is sin.

Every time you have sex with someone, you're giving them a piece of you that you can't get back. Now, when you have sex with your spouse, that part of you is a gift. However, when it's someone else, that piece of your soul is stolen—never to be returned. It's not like a favorite jacket. When the relationship ends, you can't just stop by one afternoon, endure an awkward conversation, and retrieve it. I've heard the toughest part of breaking up is getting your stuff back. And in this situation, that's definitely the case. You're giving away part of your spirit—a piece of your soul. Why would you ever trust someone with part of your soul if you're not married?

Here's the deal: sex is the physical act of marriage. The Bible calls it becoming one flesh. It is an intimate, physical, emotional, and spiritual connection. And whether you like it or not, you're connected to that person for the rest of your life. If you have sex with ten people, you're connected to ten people. Why is it like this? Because sex is meant for marriage. In a lot of ways sex *is* marriage. You're connecting your emotions, spirit, and physical self to another person. Why would you just throw that around like it's nothing?

Marriage is a legally binding contract. It attaches two people together in the eyes of the government. But more importantly, marriage is a spiritually binding contract. It attaches two people together in the eyes of God. He designed sex to strengthen the connection between a man and a woman. It ties them together. That's why it's so much harder for sexually active people to end relationships. Sex is binding. The very nature of it is to fasten people closer to one another. That's why it's so important to save sex for marriage. Sex is an incredibly deep physical, emotional, and spiritual commitment to another person. It should only happen inside a relationship that recognizes that commitment and responsibility which means marriage.

Sex, Marriage, and the Bible

So what does the Bible have to say about sex inside of marriage? The answer might surprise you.

Drink water from your own well—
    share your love only with your wife.
Why spill the water of your springs in the streets,
    having sex with just anyone?
You should reserve it for yourselves.
    Never share it with strangers.
Let your wife be a fountain of blessing for you.
    Rejoice in the wife of your youth.
She is a loving deer, a graceful doe.
    Let her breasts satisfy you always.
    May you always be captivated by her love.

Why be captivated, my son, by an immoral woman,

or fondle the breasts of a promiscuous woman?

-Proverbs 5:15-20

That's arousing language even by today's standards. And maybe God's not a prude after all. Perhaps He understands how great sex is. I mean, He did create it. Sex is a wonderful thing meant to be enjoyed and looked forward to. But it's also meant only for married people.

So what does the Bible have to say about sex outside of marriage? At this point, the answer should not surprise you.

Flee from sexual immorality. All other sins a man commits are outside his body, but he who sins sexually sins against his own body.

-1 Corinthians 6:18

God's will is for you to be holy, so stay away from all sexual sin. Then each of you will control his own body and live in holiness and honor—not in lustful passion like the pagans who do not know God and his ways.

-1 Thessalonians 4:3

Put to death, therefore, whatever belongs to your earthly nature: sexual immorality, impurity, lust, evil desires and greed, which is idolatry.

-Colossians 3:5

The acts of the sinful nature are obvious: sexual immorality, impurity and debauchery

-Galatians 5:19

It's funny how the phrase "sexual immorality" gets thrown around so much. I've heard many people call the phrase too vague. They say it doesn't necessarily include sex before marriage. Some claim it doesn't include oral sex. There are all sorts of theories about what constitutes sexual immorality, but it really just boils down to people trying to justify the sin they're committing. As Christians, there is only one way to look at it. And we all know what it is, it's just a question of buying in to it or not. First Corinthians says it best.

Now to the unmarried and the widows I say: It is good for them to stay unmarried, as I am. But if they cannot control themselves, they should marry, for it is better to marry than to burn with passion.

-1 Corinthians 7:8-9

Paul doesn't say, "If you can't control yourself, just go ahead and have sex; it's not that big of a deal." He doesn't say, "Oral sex is a good way to get around self-control." He effectively says that if you aren't strong enough to control your sexual urges then you should get married to avoid sexual sin. Marriage. Period.

Sex in the Bible is often referred to using a form of the word "know." Adam *knew* Eve his wife, Cain *knew* his wife, and so on. It's this idea that sex requires a deep knowledge of another person. And if you're not married, you don't have that knowledge. You might think you do. You might believe that you have everything figured out about your significant other. But trust me, if you married him or her tomorrow, you would find out so much more it's shocking. People don't open up completely until

95

their married, and for good reason. Marriage is a commitment for life, and without that commitment, it's unwise to share everything with another person. Why would you trust someone with your deepest and darkest if you're not sure they'll stay? Marriage is the only way to truly know someone. In other words, you should know a person as a spouse before you *know* a person as a sexual partner.

Justified

During my sophomore year I got asked to help with a big youth weekend at a friend of mine's church. Most all of the small group leaders were college students, and before the weekend events got started, we hung out and got to know each other. I met a girl there named Candace who was debating with a few others about sex before marriage. She claimed that "sexual immorality" didn't necessarily apply to sex between two unmarried people. She believed that as long as two people were planning on getting married, sex was okay. I found out a couple weeks later that Candace and her boyfriend had been having sex for a while, and my gut tells me she was feeling just a tad bit guilty over it. She was trying desperately to justify her actions.

Look, if you really want to have sex, you're going to find a way to justify it. But realize that using the Bible to justify sex is just like a slaveholder using it to justify slavery. It's just like a TV evangelist using it to justify his demands for people to send him money. It's just like a crusader using it to justify killing innocent Arab children. Does that sound too harsh? The truth usually does. It's our human nature to look at sin as having varying degrees of wrongness. Molestation is much worse than lying. Murder is much worse than stealing. And so on and so forth. We often look at sin with a mindset of the lowest common denominator. One sin doesn't seem nearly as wrong as a whole bunch of other sins, so maybe it's not so bad. However, God sees things based on the highest common denominator. In His eyes, lying is just as wrong as molesting someone; stealing is just as evil as murder. All sin is equal; all sin is heinous. If you don't like it, take it up with Him.

You can't make the Bible say what you want it to, and you can't scratch out passages because they make you feel convicted.

The most ridiculous instance of justification I've ever heard of happened in high school. A guy I knew told a girl, "Ya know, Adam and Eve weren't married when they first had sex." And it worked. That girl had sex with him. What I've found is that if a person is doing something wrong, he or she either has to stop doing it or find a way to justify it. Too often, Christians reason out sex in their minds to make it alright when it's not at all God's intention. So if you find yourself having to justify a behavior to not feel guilty about it, there's probably something wrong with what you're doing. Perhaps you should stop the behavior instead of trying to find a loophole for it. Your soul will be a lot better off.

Going Too Far

How far is too far? Really? You know the answer to this; you just don't want to believe it. (I didn't want to believe it either.) I know a lot of people who think some things are okay as long as there is no actual intercourse. It's like having abbreviated sex. But for the record, that's still sex. Oral sex, anal sex, mutual masturbation, and any variations all fall into the category of sexual contact. And to put it bluntly, it's all sinful outside of marriage. It's a bummer I know, but you'll have to take it up with God.

As Christians, we have to be especially careful about the situations we put ourselves in. Sitting on a bed with your girlfriend in a dark dorm room while watching a movie isn't exactly a smart way to avoid sexual desire. Shacking up with your boyfriend probably won't help you keep the relationship pure. Satan wants nothing more than to destroy you, and sex is one of his favorite methods. So play it smart. Don't wind up in a compromising position.

With that said, I don't see how anything past kissing can be considered okay in a Christian relationship. I understand that putting your hand up a girl's shirt or down a guy's pants feels good and isn't exactly "sex," but what do you think those things lead to? It's like opening a bag of potato chips and thinking you can eat just one. By the end of the night, the whole bag is gone. My advice is to draw the line at making out. Anything beyond that is asking for trouble. I realize how tough that can be, but anything beyond kissing is a slippery slope.

Here's the thing about pushing the envelope in a relationship: Whenever that relationship ends, the next relationship will pick up where the last one left off. So let's say you got to the point where you were taking each other's clothes off. Nothing past that, just making out with no clothes on. Then you break up. Well, the next relationship is going to jump to taking clothes off a lot quicker than last time. You've already decided that it's okay, so it's a lot easier to get to that point. Then, that justification leads to thinking that oral sex isn't *really* sex. And so on, and so on until you've gotten comfortable with everything. You might think it can't happen to you, but I've seen it turn out this way over and over again. Once you start opening these doors, you can't close them. And each door opened makes the next one even easier to go through.

For the record, no one ever goes too far on accident. That's garbage. Your hand doesn't suddenly take on a mind of its own. The wind doesn't unzip your pants. And sex faeries don't place a condom in your pocket. Everything you do sexually is a choice that you consciously make. I understand getting caught up in the moment, but you chose long before that to be alone together. It's far too common for us to set ourselves up for sin and then claim it was unintentional. Don't fall into the trap.

Pornography

Porn is so easy to get a hold of now it's ridiculous. Back in the day, a guy would find half a Playboy in a dumpster and would have to bury it to keep it safe. Now, it literally takes typing one word into Google to have access to millions upon millions of pictures and videos. Anybody with an internet connection can spend all day watching all the smut he wants. And you don't even have to go looking for it. So do yourself a favor and keep SafeSearch on.

I guess I could go into how sinful it is to watch porn, but I figure you already know that. By now I hope you understand the whole lust being bad thing, so I'm gonna focus on the other aspects of it.

It's a huge waste of time. Spending an hour watching porn and then masturbating isn't exactly the best use of sixty-one minutes. So if you ever get the urge to look up pictures of naked people, go somewhere and do something productive. Go work out. Go throw a Frisbee around. Go read a book. Go study. Go get started on that paper that's coming up. Go do anything. Just go. Get away from the desire. You'll be glad you did. (If you're really feeling crazy, you could crack open your Bible.)

It's not real. They do a good job of hiding it sometimes, but that cable repair man and girl who just stepped out of the shower don't actually exist. And they don't actually find what they're doing as pleasurable as they make it seem. They're actors being paid to act. That's all. Real sex doesn't work anything like what they show. It's all just a fantasy, and watching too much can give you a distorted view of what sex is supposed to be like.

It's addictive. Porn addiction is just as real as being addicted to drugs, alcohol, or gambling. Many people get to the point where they *need* it and have a hard time functioning without it. Marriages have been ruined, jobs have been lost, and good Christian people have been compromised because of the addictive power of pornography. Don't let it be you. Please. Don't even open up the door for the enemy to ruin you like that.

Here's the biggest thing about pornography: **once you see it, you can't unsee it**. Everything that goes into your brain stays there until you get dementia. So the more crap you put in, the more crap gets trapped in there. Guard your eyes. Guard your mind. Be careful of what you allow in. Lust has destroyed people who had much stronger faith than you and me, so don't think it can't happen.

A Final Thought

I realize that the topic of sex in Christianity often looks like just another rule or regulation. But it's not like that at all. God doesn't want people to wait until marriage just because He says so. He's not on a power trip. He wants you to wait because it's the best possible way to live. Even non-Christians should save sex for marriage.

We're wired so intricately, and sex has such an impact on that wiring that we should be careful and smart about how we approach sex. I've met so many college students who have regrets. Both Christians and non-Christians leave college wishing they could go back and change things. And so many times those regrets involve sex. Whether it was a bad decision at a party, waking up to find the other person gone, or staying in a relationship too long just because of the sex, people have experienced serious damage because of poor sexual choices. I don't want it to happen to you. I don't want you to graduate wishing you could undo something. And I especially don't want you to have to endure the strife that sex so often causes young college students.

I also realize that sex gets painted in a rather negative light sometimes. But it's truly something to look forward to and enjoy at the proper time. It may seem cruel to have to wait but I promise it's worth it. Don't think of it as a curse for unmarried people; look at it as a gift to take pleasure in with your spouse. Sex is an awesome thing when you handle it properly, but don't just take my word for it.

Young Man

You have captured my heart,
      my treasure, my bride.
You hold it hostage with one glance of your eyes,
      with a single jewel of your necklace.
Your love delights me,
      my treasure, my bride.
Your love is better than wine,
      your perfume more fragrant than spices.
Your lips are as sweet as nectar, my bride.
      Honey and milk are under your tongue.
Your clothes are scented
      like the cedars of Lebanon.
You are my private garden, my treasure, my bride,
      a secluded spring, a hidden fountain.
Your thighs shelter a paradise of pomegranates
      with rare spices—
henna with nard,
      nard and saffron,
fragrant calamus and cinnamon,
      with all the trees of frankincense, myrrh, and aloes,
and every other lovely spice.
      You are a garden fountain,
a well of fresh water
      streaming down from Lebanon's mountains.

Young Woman

Awake, north wind!
      Rise up, south wind!

Blow on my garden

>and spread its fragrance all around.

Come into your garden, my love;

>taste its finest fruits.

-Song of Solomon 4:9-16

God understands how incredible sex is, but engaging in it outside the parameters of marriage can be devastating, and I'm not even referring to STDs. By now I figure you've already seen all the ridiculous statistics on the rampancy of STDs, and you've probably had to sit through an unnerving health class slide show of the affects of STDs on reproductive systems. So I don't want to waste your time with stuff you already know. But for the record, being sexually active in college will probably lead to at least one STD according to the percentages. (Don't say I didn't warn you.)

Solomon and his wife were very much aware of how great sex is, and the language in their writing proves that. However, they kept it inside a married relationship. God isn't a prude. He gets it. But He also wants you to live the best possible life you can. Waiting to have sex is part of that.

Now, I'm not so naive to think everyone who is reading this is still a virgin. High school wasn't that long ago; I remember what all went on. And I'll be honest, if you've already had sex, your years in college are going to be pretty difficult when it comes to dealing with all the opportunities to have sex again. Sex is a door that can't be closed once it's opened, and once your body experiences it, you only want it that much more. You're going to have to really work to avoid having sex again until you're married. It's gonna require a lot of time spent in prayer, being around people who will hold you accountable, and pursuing truly pure relationships. It'll be tough, but I promise you can do it. You just have to be smart about the situations you put yourself in. Don't set yourself up to fail.

If you're currently in a relationship that has gone too far, cut all physical stuff out and see what you have left. A lot of relationships become based on sexual contact instead of anything of actual substance. It's important to not fall into that trap. One of the main reasons the divorce rate is so high is because people put too much emphasis on the physical and not enough on the things that matter like conversation, shared interests, and mutual beliefs.

If your significant other is opposed to cutting all the physical contact, perhaps you have your answer right there. I know it's hard to stop, but the future of your relationship literally depends on it. What's more valuable: the instant gratification of sex or the long-term benefits of figuring out if a relationship is truly meant to be? And just so we're clear, the whole sexual contact thing shouldn't start up again until you're married. I know it sucks. Get over it.

Honestly, you'll probably slip up a few times. Sex is an extremely hard habit to break. Just keep fighting. Keep praying for strength. And surround yourself with people who are also trying to stay abstinent. It's going to be difficult. I don't want to disillusion you into thinking this is going to be easy. It'll truly be one of the hardest things you've ever done. But you CAN do it. And I promise the reward is better than you can imagine.

If you're still a virgin, you won't have an absolutely easy time remaining one, but the longer you hold out the better you'll get at saying no. Staying a virgin until marriage is no small feat in this day and age, but I want you to know that it IS possible. Never buy the lie that everyone is doing it. That's garbage. You're probably in the minority, but keep your head up. The light at the end of the tunnel is much brighter for those who stay pure. You might even run into people who admire you for your self-control.

***

College life presents extraordinary challenges when it comes to your physical self. A lack of parental control combined with curiosity, rebellion, and constant opportunity creates some tough situations to navigate. I'll be up front about this: college is a lot easier if you're not a Christian. If you have no desire to love God, there's no such thing as temptation. If you have no desire to love people, it doesn't matter what happens at parties and in your dorm room. And if the cliché college life is more important to you than God, then so be it. That's your choice.

If you think the sex, drugs, and alcohol are better than Him, then feel free to live out the next few years as you please. However, if you find that God means more to you than the empty "pleasures" of this world, then live like it. If the One who carved the mountains and dug the oceans—who loves you more than anything and sent His Son to die to prove that love—truly matters to you, then act in a way that brings Him glory.

There is no grey area. Either having sex with your girlfriend is important or God is important. Either getting wasted on the weekends is important or God is important. Either porn, or weed, or pursuing casual encounters is important to you or God is. You can't have the sin of this world and God. It doesn't work that way. You have to choose.

So what's your choice?

6. Mental

Do not conform any longer to the pattern of this world, but be transformed by the renewing of your mind. Then you will be able to test and approve what God's will is—his good, pleasing and perfect will.

-Romans 12:2

We often forget the "with all your mind" part.

Love the Lord your God with all your heart and with all your soul and with all your strength and with all your mind

-Luke 10:27

Maybe it's because it comes last. Whatever the case, we tend to neglect what is equally as important as heart, soul, and strength. And college presents some awesome opportunities to transform and renew your mind. You just have to take advantage of them.

Class

You're obviously going to spend a ton of time in class while in college. (Hopefully) And you're going to learn some remarkable stuff. You're also going to have to make some tough decisions about how what you're learning compares to your faith.

A lot of Christians shy away from certain classes because

they're afraid of learning something that might make them doubt God. That's understandable, and if your faith is still shaky, that's probably a good idea. However, if all it takes is one class and one professor to shatter your faith in God—in your belief that Jesus is who He says He is—then your faith was probably bogus to begin with. I'm not saying you won't have doubt, but it should take a lot more than one college class to make you give up on God. I hope your faith is strong enough to encounter everything your classes can throw at it.

Take hard courses. Don't run from them. Christians have trouble with science and philosophy classes in particular, and many simply avoid them. But that's not the best plan of action.

Test everything. Hold on to the good.

-1 Thessalonians 5:21

Find out different viewpoints; see what the other side is saying. Then test it. And I can't stress **test it** enough. A lot of Christians take college classes and believe everything a professor says. Now, it's good to have an open mind, but don't keep it so open that you buy in to a bunch of garbage. Just because your professor has a PhD doesn't mean she's right. Test what you're being told. Decide for yourself what works and what doesn't. Hold on to the good.

Science

It's hilarious to me that people think science disproves God. They think that finding out how something works or where it originated shows that God didn't have a hand in it. Yet, the more we "figure out," the more life points to a divine construction. It's all about your perspective.

For by him all things were created: things in heaven and on earth, visible and invisible, whether thrones or powers or rulers or authorities; all things were created by him and for him. He is before all things, and in him all things hold together.

-Colossians 1:16-17

Paul is saying that not only did Jesus make the universe, He is also the glue that holds it all together. With that in mind, it's no wonder creation is so awe-inspiring. Take gravity for instance. Before Isaac Newton figured it out, people just thought God's power kept everything from floating away. That's pretty straightforward, and it's a simple way of looking at the world. However, after Newton, we learned that gravity was keeping everything grounded. Then we learned that gravity had a specific speed. Then all sorts of equations spawned from that. So the idea of what kept us from floating away went from the incredibly simple idea of "God did it" to the extraordinarily complex idea that there is a force that acts and reacts in specific ways, and there are mathematical equations that go along with it. While one perspective suggests that this discovery disproves God, I say it proves divine creation even more. It's as if gravity was painstakingly engineered.

Many Christians have trouble with evolution. But if evolution is proven to be how we all got here, I don't see how that changes anything. If God created a constantly changing and evolving planet, why wouldn't he create constantly changing and evolving organisms? The story in Genesis and evolution might even go hand in hand. People assume that the word "day" means a twenty-four hour period. But in Jewish culture, a day doesn't have a set length; it runs from sunset to sunset. So it's very possible that each day in the creation story could have lasted millions of years. That's the blink of an eyelid to God. And while we're on the subject, the sun and moon didn't come along until day four, which makes the idea of "day" during creation even more interesting. So could it be that God used evolution to create man? Perhaps. I think it's certainly possible. But if there's one thing I've learned through research on the subject, no one really knows how and why it all went down. There are some good theories from both sides, but it's all a bunch of guessing.

At the same time, don't hide behind the idea of "God did it." Using "God did it" as the reason for why something happens isn't incorrect, but it is a religious copout. If you really want to transform and renew your mind, learn how the universe works. Find out all the intricate details. Many people will tell you that these "findings" show God's absence. I think they show us a universe so full of God it's bursting at the seams. Just because man figures out how and why something happens doesn't mean God had less of a hand in it. Once again, test everything. Don't be scared of learning all there is to know about the world around you. You'll be surprised how often you find God. And His attention to detail will blow you away.

Philosophy

Philosophy classes give nearly all Christians problems. There are a ton of ideas that just seem to be right when you first look at them. Relativism, moralism, post-modernism, etc. all have some really enticing parts, and professors aren't always quick to point out what's wrong with them. Yet again, test everything. When you really dive in to philosophy, you start seeing holes. For instance, any philosophy that claims there is no truth just disproved itself because if the statement that there is no truth is true, then there is truth. You're going to run across all sorts of stuff like that. You're going to have some awfully convincing professors; be a skeptic. They're without question going to be skeptical of your beliefs; why not be just as skeptical of theirs?

If you run into an idea that you're not sure about, go to the Bible. What does it say? Once again, have an open mind but not one that is so open that crappy philosophy and false ideas get into it. Compare what you're hearing in class to what Jesus said. Who has more authority: your professor or Jesus?

Do some reading on Christian apologetics. (Apologetics means speaking in defense.) After 2000 years, there are very few new arguments against Christianity. Researching apologetics will help you answer the objections to your faith. So read as much as you can. Learn what great theologians think about the faith. Yet, once again, test everything. Just because a theologian has five degrees and has published thirty books doesn't mean she can't be wrong. Test it. See if it works. Make sure it fits what the Bible says.

One of the main things you need to understand about philosophy 101 classes is that the professor probably doesn't want to be there. And because of that, two types of personalities tend to emerge. The professor will either be apathetic to your thoughts, opinions, and beliefs, or he'll try to have a little fun by offending you. After years of teaching, professors know all the right things to say to get a Christian riled up. And if you don't realize that's what is happening, it's really easy to get upset and start yelling. So it's important to understand the situation going in. You can debate until you're blue in the face, but you're not going to change how a professor or classmate thinks. There is no theorem or formula that is going to change their minds. And they're more than likely pushing your buttons because they get a kick out of it. But if you know that ahead of time, it makes philosophy classes a lot easier to navigate.

Honestly, I suggest you wait until at least sophomore year to tackle philosophy classes. Freshmen are naturally pretty impressionable, and it's easy for an experienced professor to mislead an untrained mind. I've known a number of really grounded Christians that gave up on God after taking philosophy courses during freshman year. Their faith just wasn't strong enough to combat the objections made by teachers and classmates. So wait until you really understand what and why you believe; then, hit those classes full force. It's important to hear arguments against what you believe. Hearing the other side makes you think about your faith in new ways and will help develop a mature belief system.

You're probably going to run into times when you start questioning your faith. Just remember that God is a big boy; He can handle it. I think He wants us to seriously think about our faith and relationship with Him. But when a class or professor starts putting doubt in your mind, it's important to go back to the foundations of what you believe. When a new idea starts messing with you, contemplate how it truly affects your life. Does it change the fact that Jesus died for you? Does it change why you accepted Christ as your savior? Does this new idea really shake your beliefs to the core or is it just another superficial thought that is being presented by a charismatic and clever person?

When you start wondering what to believe, go back to the basics of your faith and work your way back out. Don't assume some goober in a bowtie knows what he's talking about.

See to it that no one takes you captive through hollow and deceptive philosophy, which depends on human tradition and the basic principles of this world rather than on Christ.

-Colossians 2:8

Christian Classes

Most schools have religion departments that offer a plethora of courses dealing with Christianity. Take them. Learn as much as you can. Like any other class however, there are plenty of lies floating around, so don't just assume everything your professor says is true. Keep in mind that the professors who teach these classes aren't always Christians.

With that said, don't sign up for these classes looking for a Bible study. Religion courses in college are designed to feed your brain not your heart. If you go in looking for an emotional outcome, you'll be sorely disappointed. However, you're liable to learn a lot more than you would expect. Pastors and youth directors don't usually focus on the history and culture of Christianity and the Bible, so these classes are great opportunities to learn how it all came together. One of the most enlightening college classes I ever took concentrated on women in the Hebrew Scriptures and gave me a whole new perspective on stories I had known since I was a kid.

You'll probably learn some things that make you question your faith. There are a ton of Biblical scholars and they don't all agree. Some think certain books of the Bible weren't written by who they're attributed to. Some don't think the miracles actually happened. Some think the original words have been severely altered. You're likely to find out some very interesting theories and ideas about Jesus and the Bible. Test everything. Don't jump to a conclusion without hearing all sides and knowing all the facts. Look at how God has worked in your own life. Then make a decision about what to believe.

Arguments and debates in Christian courses tend to get more intense than in any other class.

But avoid foolish debates, genealogies, quarrels, and disputes about the law, for they are unprofitable and worthless.

-Titus 3:9

Yelling and arguing in a Christian class is useless. And keep in mind that it's one of the Devil's favorite things to watch. Countless churches split up every year over what are really unimportant issues, and relationships fall apart all the time because of frivolous debates. All these heated quarrels do is instigate anger and aggravation. Having a peaceful conversation about controversial topics can be an incredibly enlightening thing, but when tempers start to flare and the focus of the discussion is no longer love, it's time to find something else to do. It's okay for people to believe differently than you. It shows your spiritual maturity when you either remain calm and respectful or get angry and antagonistic. Also, remember that Christianity is not about winning arguments, so if you want to be a master debater, do me a favor and keep it to yourself.

I highly recommend taking classes on Christianity, but be careful of pitfalls and falsehoods. Be skeptical; don't buy in too quickly. And don't be afraid to talk out ideas with other Christians and people in the class. Just avoid getting into arguments. This is all part of the process of figuring out your faith.

Answers

Always be prepared to give an answer to everyone who asks you to give the reason for the hope that you have.

-1 Peter 3:15

Be prepared to defend yourself. College can be pretty hostile towards Christianity. Professors and classmates might talk down to you and try to prove your faith to be ridiculous. Just think of these times as opportunities to grow in love and patience. Getting mad or offended is not going to help your case. As I said earlier, it's important to realize when people are simply trying to make you angry. So, whenever someone attacks what you believe, remain calm and try to answer their objections the best you can. You're not going to have all the answers, and it's okay to say "I don't know."

With that said, it's important for you to figure out why you believe what you believe. I knew a couple people in my dorm who were Catholic. During Lent, they would eat fish on Fridays. But when I asked them why, none of them could give me a real reason. It was just something they had always done. One of them called and asked her parents, but they didn't know either. Wow. Really? For one thing, a tradition is empty and devoid of all meaning if you don't understand why you do it. And even worse, it really looked bad on their faith. If you don't know why you believe what you believe, then how can you expect others to believe it?

So if you believe Jesus is the way, truth, and life, why do you believe it? Is Jesus the only path to salvation? How could you possibly believe in a God?

You're going to have to answer these and much harder questions, so I suggest that you go ahead and figure out some answers. What's your testimony? I mean, why are you a Christian in the first place? Have you thought about it? People are gonna ask. Get ready.

Part of loving God with all your mind is understanding *why* you love God with all your mind, and each person will have a different answer. For some it's because of a tragic situation that ended in triumph. For others it has to do with experiencing nature. For me it's because I've been a part of so many things that just can't be explained by coincidence. I've seen God show up so many times that I can't help but have a relationship with Him. And whenever someone asks me about it, I've got a ton of stories to back it up.

[S]top thinking like children. In regard to evil be infants, but in your thinking be adults.

-1 Corinthians 14:20

So it's time to grow up. It's time to see how truly complex and complicated God is. It's time to figure out your faith and be able to explain why it's yours. Don't be a Christian lightweight; don't be one of those people who can't explain his beliefs. When someone questions you, it's important to have something to tell them. You won't know the answer to everything, but you can at least know the main concepts of Christianity and why you believe in certain traditions. And hopefully you have some stories that show how God is working in your life. It's time to claim the faith as your own. No more believing it because it's what you've always done. Just as it's time for you to be an adult, it's time for your faith to mature as well.

New Facts Have Come to Light

If your faith hinges on one idea so much that if that one thing is disproven, your entire faith falls apart, then I have to question how strong your faith was to begin with. And that goes for anything, not just God.

If a scientist puts faith in a hypothesis and thinks if she adds X and Y then she's going to get Z, I doubt she will do just one experiment. If in that first test, she adds X and Y and gets K, it's highly unlikely—if she's worth the degree on her wall—that she'll just call it a day. She won't call the faith in her hypothesis misguided after just one or two or maybe even a hundred experiments. She's going to continue to research, test, and study until her hypothesis is proven right or proven beyond a shadow of a doubt to be wrong. Why not approach faith in God the same way?

A lot of people treat faith like a stack of blocks. They put all their ideas about faith one on top of the other. So if they remove one block, if they find out one idea was wrong, then all the blocks above it topple too.

So let's say you've grown up your entire life believing the Earth is only 6000 years old. Then, you get to college and find out archeologists have found fossils dated back over a million years. Now, if your faith is stacked on the idea that the planet is only a few thousand years old, then one little fossil can cause the entire thing to crumble. But if that's the case—if one new discovery can blow your house down—then how strong was that faith in the first place?

I've got a youth director friend named Jeremy who looks at faith a different way. He sees it more like a giant spider web. God is at the center, and all your ideas about Him make up the rest of the web. The great thing about a spider web is that you can remove part of it and the whole thing doesn't collapse. So let's say you're struggling with the idea of the trinity. Then, take it out of the web, roll it around, spin it in different ways, and try to figure it out. But while this is going on, the web stays intact. Questions about the age of the earth or the trinity don't affect other parts of your faith, so why would they tear down the whole thing?

Your relationship with God shouldn't be built on a wobbly foundation; when new facts come to light, your entire faith shouldn't crumble and fall.

Knowledge vs. Knowing

There's a huge difference between having knowledge of something and knowing something. I can read books and listen to podcasts about cooking which will give me great knowledge on the subject of preparing food. However, I will never *know* cooking until I step into the kitchen and turn on the stove. I can watch Youtube videos about painting for days on end, but until I put a brush to canvas, I'll never know art. Just because you know about something doesn't mean you know it—especially when it comes to God.

Just because you know a lot *about* God doesn't mean you know God. Being knowledgeable on the subject of Jesus doesn't mean you know Him as lord and savior. There are plenty of people in Hell who knew everything there was to know about Christ but because they never knew Him personally, all that knowledge was useless.

In your pursuit of knowledge—in your Bible studies, courses

on religion, and books about Jesus—don't neglect your relationship with God. It's really easy to get wrapped up in the thought of God and forget about the actual God. Be careful of chasing after knowledge and losing sight of why you're seeking. Don't let knowledge of God become a god. It resembles the real thing but can't actually satisfy. Knowledge is only a means to an end. Don't confuse it with what truly matters. If you're not in relationship with God—if you're not seeking Him, and doing your absolute best to follow Him with every aspect of your life—then all the knowledge in the world won't save you.

Don't get me wrong, having knowledge of God is extremely important. You should learn as much about Him as you possibly can. However, *knowing* God is all that counts. There's no multiple choice test to get in to Heaven. There's only a testing of the heart. Either God has it or the world has it. I think you know how it all goes down from there.

So do you just have knowledge of God, or do you actually know God? Do you just know all the stories, Bible verses, and commandments, or are you in actual relationship with Him?

7. Lip Service

The greatest single cause of atheism in the world today is Christians, who acknowledge Jesus with their lips and walk out the door, and deny Him by their lifestyle. That is what an unbelieving world simply finds unbelievable.

-Brennan Manning

A lot of people get mad when they hear someone say "God damn." I don't blame them as it's a completely unacceptable thing to say. However, I believe lip service to be on a totally different level of taking the Lord's name in vain.

Saying GD is a quick outburst, but lip service—perhaps better known as hypocrisy—is a lifestyle. So every day a person, who claims to love God, doesn't follow through with his actions is a day lived taking His name in vain. It is what we do that defines us, not what we say. And Christians who give God nothing but lip service are Satan's greatest allies. Not only do these people damage themselves and spoil their own relationships with God, but they also keep non-Christians from realizing who God is.

Be About It

The one who says he remains in Him should walk just as He walked.

-1 John 2:6

Don't just talk about it. Be about it. If you claim to be a Christian, then you have to walk as Jesus walked. There is no grey area here. You can't say one thing and your life prove something completely different. It's one thing to make mistakes; I mean we're all hypocrites at one time or another; but if your choices on a daily basis don't reflect Christ, then you're not actually a Christian. Talking a good game has no place in the kingdom of God.

While I was playing football, a new coach was hired to the staff. When he first got there, he showed us a PowerPoint presentation to give a little background as to who he was and how he coached. Coach Jerome showed us highlights of how well his system worked at his previous school. He read us quotes that influenced his life. He showed us a picture of his daughter and talked about how much she mattered to him. But what really got my attention was Jerome talking about how important faith and God were to him. When he said that, I thought "awesome." Here's a guy I can trust. Here's a coach who won't cuss players out and will treat people with the respect they deserve.

Over the next few months, I found out what was *really* important to Jerome. It became apparent that the only thing he was actually concerned with was adding zeroes to the end of his paycheck. He put players down. He cussed out a different guy every day. Whenever someone asked him a question he didn't know the answer to, Jerome would speak loudly and talk down to the player to try to cover up his lack of knowledge. It became obvious that the whole "faith and God being important to him" thing was really just lip service.

One of my really good friends on the team was coming off major shoulder surgery and no one expected him to play. While my friend recovered, Coach Jerome made a habit of making snide comments toward him and seemed to enjoy being disrespectful at my friend's expense. A few months later my friend defied the odds and won a starting position. And the next day, wouldn't you know it, Coach Jerome was trying to be his best friend.

Now, for a non-Christian, that kind of behavior would be expected. But for a self-proclaimed Christian to treat people like that is the definition of spiritual bankruptcy. And it's offensive to people who actually live out Christianity and don't just talk about it.

Not long ago, I was listening to a football game on the radio. During the post game show, after my former team had won, they talked to Coach Jerome. The first thing out of his mouth was, "Ya know, I just thank God for this team and this group of guys." As soon as I heard this, I laughed out loud. What a joke. And it sounds so good. It's exactly what people want to hear and I'm sure a ton of people listening to the radio that night thought good of him just like I first did. But his actions tell a very different story.

So do me a huge favor and don't be like Coach Jerome. Don't claim to be a Christian and then have your actions prove the complete opposite. That kind of thing can really screw things up for the Christians trying to change the world for the better.

The one who says, "I have come to know Him," without keeping his commands, is a liar, and the truth is not in him.

-1 John 2:4

Following Through

Christianity is all about the follow through. Reading your Bible, going to church, telling people about Jesus, and talking about how much you love God are all really great things. But if you don't back it up with how you live, then your faith is full of crap.

[W]e must not love in word or speech, but in deed and truth.

-1 John 3:18

Do you tell God you love Him? Or do you show God you love Him? Do you tell people you love them? Or do you show people you love them?

You can't bullcrap God. He knows if your actions don't line up with your speech. He's well aware if you're just putting on a show. No matter what you say, your choices are going to confirm who you really are. You can't just love God with your words; you can't just follow Jesus in your heart. You have to go out and show your love with your life. There's no such thing as a Christian who talks it without walking it. Words don't carry a cross. A bunch of letters strung together don't help a dying world. Your life has to reflect what you're saying.

Do you know anybody who is a really great Christian on Sundays? She goes to church, she always brings her Bible, she knows all the words to the worship songs, and she listens intently as the pastor preaches. But from Monday to Saturday, she lives like Sunday never happened. Have you met people like that?

Do not merely listen to the word, and so deceive yourselves. Do what it says.

-James 1:22

Think of Christianity as an action verb. Being part of it requires a lot more than sitting in a pew on Sunday mornings or attending a Bible study on Wednesday nights. You can't just hear and read the word. You have to do what it says. Your life shouldn't look different from Sunday to Monday.

With that said, if God is leading you to do something or go somewhere, you should heed that calling. And when I say "should," I mean that we're required to go where God tells us.

If we live by the spirit, we must also follow the Spirit.

-Galatians 5:25

Claiming to be a Christian but not following the Spirit is just as much lip service as a Christian treating people like garbage. Once again, you can't declare one thing and then live out another. So, if you've chosen to live by the Spirit, go where it leads.

A Final Note

College offers daily opportunities to turn your faith into lip service. You'll have plenty of chances to claim to be a Christian and then live otherwise. Whether you're at a party, in a class, or in a dorm room by yourself, you'll have tough decisions to make about the person you want to be and the life you want to lead. I hope your walk matches your talk. I hope you realize that a real relationship with Jesus is a lot better than a pretend one. I hope you'll not only read the Bible but that you'll also do what it says. I hope you'll follow where the Holy Spirit leads you. And if you choose to not do those things, I hope you won't tell anyone you're a Christian because honestly, you're not. So, may your actions speak louder than your words.

Preach the Gospel at all times and when necessary use words.

-St. Francis of Assisi

8. Trials

"At the Gate of the Year"

"I said to the man who stood at the gate of the year

'Give me a light that I may tread safely into the unknown.'

And he replied, 'Go into the darkness and put your hand into the hand of God.

That shall be to you better than light and safer than a known way!'"

-Minnie Louise Harkins

Trials will define your college career. The hard times of the next few years will expose who you really are and reveal exactly where your faith is. Relationships will splinter; someone close to you will die; parents will have problems; professors will be unbearable; friends will betray you; and life will come out of nowhere to knock you down.

Remember this: **Life is not about what happens to you. It's how you deal with what happens that matters.**

Most of the trials that come your way will be out of your control. However, you have complete control over how you react to the crap life throws at you. Understand that college moves in cycles. You'll go weeks without anything going on, and then all of a sudden your world will collapse for three days straight. You might get slammed with four tests on the same day or three twelve page research papers due by noon on Tuesday. You might have a huge internship interview the day after your significant other decides it's "just not working out." Your best friend might start dating the guy or girl that just broke up with you, and they might reveal their relationship by making out at your birthday party. You might even find yourself spiraling into a deep pit of darkness. (Perhaps that's a bit too dramatic.)

My point is that trials are coming. You're going to face difficulty in the classroom, on a sports field, in your relationships, in your mind, and pretty much everywhere else. You will face pain and strife that you can't even imagine, but how you respond to these hardships will determine who you really are. And through it all, you'll have a choice to make. Either you cut ties with God, or you lean on Him more. It's up to you.

It's so easy to be faithful when life is good. But it's during the trials that you really learn how strong your faith is. Let's be honest, when life gets hard, most people turn and run. It's a lot easier to just blame God or give up on faith. But it's the ones who stick it out who see the Kingdom. There's nothing wrong with being afraid or unsure during a stressful time. You just have to stand your ground and fight through the storm.

You've probably already seen a fair amount of trials, but get ready. More are on the way. And through them, you'll find out just what you're made of.

Temptation

We all have our weaknesses. There's something in each of us that the Devil can use to entice us away from God. And college, it seems, is a perfect time to do it. You better believe the enemy is going to do everything he can to get you to turn your back on the Creator of the universe. That's his thing. It's what he does. Throughout the next four years, you'll have all sorts of opportunities to choose a side. And it *is* a choice by the way. You can claim that "God made me this way" junk if you want to, but you choose how this all plays out. If you think something else is more valuable than God, then so be it. But before you make that choice, I hope you look into all the facts.

When tempted, no one should say, "God is tempting me." For God cannot be tempted by evil, nor does he tempt anyone; but each one is tempted when, by his own evil desire, he is dragged away and enticed. Then, after desire has conceived, it gives birth to sin; and sin, when it is full-grown, gives birth to death.

-James 1:13-15

So, first of all, God has nothing to do with what is tempting you. Darkness cannot survive being anywhere close to God, so whatever sin is enticing you comes straight from the selfishness that broods inside of you. That's why the "God made me this way" argument is a bunch of crap. As Americans, we really like to pass the blame. Whether it's a car accident, spilling hot coffee, or getting fat, we make sure someone else gets blamed and pays for it.

As a culture, we aren't very good at removing the planks from our own eyes. Yet, according to God, the blame falls squarely on each of our shoulders. So no matter what temptation you're dealing with, accept the fact that it's on you. Saying it's God's or someone else's fault is just an excuse. No one forces your hand without your permission.

Second of all, temptation is the first stage in separation from God, and surrendering to selfish desire allows Satan to get his hands on you. That may sound a little intense, and I realize we live in an age where the Devil doesn't get as much credit as he used to, but believe it or not, he still exists. He continues to lurk around like a lion waiting to devour you. All he needs is an opening. Entertaining temptation opens the door for Satan to sink his teeth into you, and then the battle is on. And either you'll fight your way back to the light, or you'll convince yourself that the sin isn't so bad.

I doubt many would argue against the fact that any and every temptation can be found somewhere on a college campus. Truly, any desire imaginable can be satisfied if you know where to look. And make no mistake, many of your classmates are giving in to temptation on a daily basis. However, as followers of Jesus, we're called to live lives of value, not ones that seek out earthly pleasures. But it's all about your perspective. Too often, as Christians, we look at temptation as a big list of rules. We turn it into a bunch of regulations that govern our lives and keep us from having too much fun. But that's not how it is at all.

It's not about saying "no" to temptation, it's about saying "yes" to Christ. Don't turn it into a catalog of no's. No sex before marriage; no drugs; no underage drinking; no cheating; no backstabbing; and so on. All that does is turn Christianity into religion. But this has *never* been about religion. Christianity has *always* been about the relationship with God. Don't think of it as what all you have to say no to. Look at it as an unbelievable, improbable, undeserved opportunity to say YES to a God who loves us for no good reason.

The cure for temptation is focus.

Therefore, submit to God. But resist the Devil, and he will flee from you. Draw near to God, and He will draw near to you.

-James 4:7-8

When you're focused on God—when you're drawing near to Him—it's impossible for temptation to overtake you. I'm not saying you won't encounter it. No matter where you go, temptation will be there to greet you with open arms. The only way to get away from it is to leave the world. Yet, I'm sure living on the moon would still have its fair share. And in college, you're going to run into temptation on a daily basis, I assure you. But if you're actively seeking God, that temptation won't be nearly as appealing to you. That girl, that guy, that money, that alcohol, that whatever will pale in comparison to the One who lives in marvelous light.

I say then, walk by the spirit and you will not carry out the desire of the flesh.

-Galatians 5:16

Desire is pretty constant. You'll always have something pulling you away from your relationship with God. As I sit here typing this, part of me wants to write hateful letters to the people who have wronged me; another part wants me to look up naked ladies on the internet. There is a battle raging in my mind over what I think is worth more: the pleasures of this world or my relationship with God. And I've found that the more I pursue God, the stronger the temptations get. It's funny how that works. And every day, I have to choose what I think is more valuable.

No temptation has overtaken you that is not common to man. God is faithful, and he will not let you be tempted beyond your ability, but with the temptation he will also provide the way of escape, that you may be able to endure it.

-1 Corinthians 10:13

You have a lot more power than you realize. Any temptation, no matter how daunting it seems, can be overcome. There is always a way out. Always. A lot of times we don't like to acknowledge the escape route; we would much rather give in to the sin and console ourselves with the "no way out" excuse. But that's garbage. God always provides a getaway. You just have to be bold enough to take it.

And what are you being tempted by anyway? Sex, money, alcohol, comfort? Have people not been dealing with all those things for thousands of years? Sure, things have changed over the years, but the core problems are the same. Nothing is going to tempt you that isn't common to every other person on this planet. But that also means that there's nothing that can tempt you that hasn't already been overcome. For years, regular people have been able to overcome exactly what is tempting you right now. Why can't you do it?

Sin is choosing something else over God. Temptation is the middleman.

It always comes down to choice. Is the sin more important to you than God? That's the question. Some people look at sin like gambling. Yeah, the odds aren't good, but there's a chance you could win big. Just let it all ride and hope the sin turns out to be more valuable than God. But trust me when I tell you it's not even close to a gamble. Gambling suggests that you could potentially walk away with more than what you came in with. But giving in to temptation will always leave you empty handed. Always. It will always be a letdown when you compare it to God.

Even Jesus was given the opportunity to give in to greed and power. But He didn't take the bait. He knew what was more important. To truly follow Him is to fight temptation no matter what the cost. I know how good that sin looks. I know how enjoyable it would be. I understand how simple it is to just reach out and take it. I get all of that. But God is worth so much more. Focus on Him. Figure out ways to better your relationship with Him. Pursue Him with everything that is in you. Don't give in to the world. The price is much too high.

Failure

College is a great time to start embracing failure. I'm not saying you should wallow in it or enjoy it, but it's important to view failure for what it is. Failure is nothing. It's breakfast. It's the price of admission to real life. Failure must be endured to truly appreciate success. Honestly, without failure, there would be no success. You have to experience a rainy day to fully grasp how great a sunny day is. To know one without knowing the other is impossible.

Failure is practice.

My great concern is not whether you have failed, but whether you are content with your failure.

-Abraham Lincoln

In college, failure just comes with the territory. It's almost guaranteed that you'll fail some tests. There's a good chance you'll fail a class. And rest assured, you'll have some relationships fail. There will be times when you put your heart and soul into something and come up empty handed. You are going to fail over and over and over again, but it's how you deal with those failures that will determine how successful you become.

The world views failure as one of the worst things that can happen. The fear of it is a driving force throughout our society. It's one of those things everyone tries to avoid at all costs. We do our best to tiptoe up the mountain to avoid falling into the valley. The last thing we would ever want to be labeled is "failures." Some people spend their whole lives so afraid to fail that they never truly live. Others become so devastated by failure that they refuse to ever try again.

Failure can turn the most promising of people into mere shells of their former selves. I know because it happened to me. I had put five years into a goal. I had poured every ounce of time, energy, and effort into it. I did everything that was necessary to achieve it. I sacrificed nearly everything to see it come to fruition. But when the time came for me to realize that dream, a set of poor circumstances and a couple people claiming to be Christians made sure all that work was for nothing. Whoever said "hard work always pays off" was misguided. In man's world, hard work can be a crapshoot. And even though I had plenty of people telling me how well I had done, even though I had accomplished a great deal, I still fell short of my goal, and I couldn't help but feel like a complete failure. Five years of work. For nothing.

Because of that failure, many of my relationships went to crap. My relationship with God hit an especially low level. And I became someone I'm not proud to look back on. Now, I could have very easily just stopped trying. I could have stopped taking risks and lived a very safe, quiet, and predictable life. But that's the opposite of what Jesus has called us to do.

Failure is a magnificent teacher. But you have to be willing to learn. Failing sucks, but there is always something to be gained from it.

What was done to me, created me.

–V for Vendetta

Every experience, every misstep, every triumph, and every failure comes together to make you in to who God wants you to be. When you fail, the world is going to see you as weak. Just remember that God uses the weak to lead the strong.

I delight in weaknesses, in insults, in hardships, in persecutions, in difficulties. For when I am weak, then I am strong.

-2 Corinthians 12:10

To fail is to live life at full speed. Being unafraid to fail is being unafraid to put your trust in God. Remember that hard work always pays off in God's world. It often takes time to see how a brutal failure can be turned into anything positive, but I assure you He knows what He's doing.

Far better is it to dare mighty things, to win glorious triumphs, even though checkered by failure... than to rank with those poor spirits who neither enjoy nor suffer much, because they live in a gray twilight that knows not victory nor defeat.

-Theodore Roosevelt

On Friday, Jesus was the biggest failure the world had ever known. He was placed in a tomb and labeled a defeated man. But on Sunday…

We live for Sunday.

In the Thick of It

I've heard a couple people say that it's during the middle of a trial that a person is truly alive. They found that when life got the hardest was when their truest selves came out. In college, you're going to have some opportunities to see your true self. It might only be a couple times; it may happen every semester. But there will be moments when life overtakes you, and you'll have to make decisions on where your trust is.

Be joyful in hope, patient in affliction, faithful in prayer.

-Romans 12:12

Is your trust in yourself or in God? Seriously. If your best friend stabs you in the back, what do you do? If another friend comes along, grabs the knife, and twists, who do you turn to? When you're in the thick of it, do you stop reading your Bible, or read it that much more? Do you give up praying, or make more time for conversations with God? Do you try to find the quickest, easiest fix to your problems, or do you remain patient and allow God to work? Do you just give up, or find joy in hope?

It's important to have these questions answered before you find yourself in the center of a storm. Too often Christians wait until the last minute to do what they should have been doing all along. They don't go to their Bibles, pray, or seek help until the dam breaks and water rushes in on them. They set themselves up to fail. It's like a sailor not doing anything to prepare for a cyclone. Then, in the final hour, when the tidal waves are bearing down on him, he tries to sure up the sails and asks the captain where the life jackets are. (Yeah, that's gonna turn out well.) Don't allow the calms of life to lull you to sleep. You'll just get owned when the storm rolls in.

Prepare during the calms to conquer the storms. Don't wait until you're in the thick of it to dust off your Bible. Don't wait for life to cave in before you start having meaningful conversations with God. And don't wait until you step in a big pile of the world's crap before you find a solid Christian you can have an honest discussion with. Don't set yourself up to fail.

It should be like muscle memory for your spirit. Reading your Bible, praying, and being patient through affliction need to become so natural to you that they happen without you even thinking about them. That way when you're going through hell, and you're exhausted and ready to just give in, that muscle memory kicks in to get you trough to the other side. But it's all about preparation. Joy comes with the morning, but how soon that morning comes often depends on how well you prepared.

The will to win is important, but the will to prepare is vital.

-Joe Paterno

It doesn't matter if you're on a sports field, in the classroom, or simply traversing the rigors of everyday life. You have to prepare, and prepare well, if you want to be successful.

Consider it a great joy whenever you experience various trials, knowing that the testing of your faith produces endurance. But endurance must do its complete work, so that you may be mature and complete, lacking nothing.

-James 1:2-4

It's amazing how often Christians get discouraged or mad at God when a trial comes along. I mean, did they think life was going to be all sunshine and roses? Did they expect God to send down unicorns to poop out happiness over the rest of their days? Let's get one thing straight: **Christianity is the hardest thing you will ever do.**

It requires sacrifice after sacrifice. And there's a good chance you'll have to endure challenges that your non-Christian friends could only dream of. But the reward is unimaginable. That's why you should take great joy when you experience trials. When God allows hardship into your life, it's because He knows you can make it through, and He wants you to become more complete in your faith. It's impossible for your faith to become more mature without trials. Faith doesn't just magically become more complete over time. To gain endurance, it has to face adversity.

There is always something to be gained from tough times. It might be patience. It could be confidence. It's often a stronger relationship with God. But whatever the case, we endure hardship for a reason. Nothing happens by chance, and it might take years to see the big picture. But just as we don't serve a trivial God, we also don't go through trivial trials. When you're in the thick of things, it's often hard to see how any good could ever come from it. But rest assured, that's when God does His finest work. So smile when life takes a shot at you. It's an opportunity to become more like Jesus.

God has marvelous ways of taking our worst tragedies and turning them into His most glorious triumphs.

-Joseph Stowell

Blessed

Dear friends, do not be surprised at the painful trial you are suffering, as though something strange were happening to you.

-1 Peter 4:12

Not only should you smile when trials come along, but you should also feel no surprise when they arrive. There shouldn't be any of that "why me" garbage. Why not you? If you say "why me" for the bad stuff, you have to say it for all the good stuff too.

You're not exactly the first person to experience a painful situation. And as a Christian, you shouldn't be shocked when life takes a dump on your front porch. It's kind of part of the deal. When you choose to not be of the world, the world doesn't exactly take it lying down. So why would you ever be surprised by a painful trial? A Christian is the enemy of the world, and you will be treated as such. But...(and there's always a but in a situation like this)

You will have suffering in this world. Be courageous! I have conquered the world.

-John 16:33

Jesus conquered the world. He took some hits, suffered some cheap shots, and was even put out of commission for a few days, but He rose to overcome the world on our behalf. So be courageous. Don't run from adversity. Stare it down, and smile as it approaches.

If the world hates you, keep in mind that it hated Me first. If you belonged to the world, it would love you as its own. As it is, you do not belong to the world, but I have chosen you out of the world. That is why the world hates you.

-John 15:18-20

Is it not a comfort for the world to hate you? Do you take pride in being able to suffer as Christ suffered? Because it's a privilege and a downright honor to endure scrutiny, affliction, and suffering for His sake. It shows us to be chosen. It shows us to be heirs.

The Spirit himself testifies with our spirit that we are God's children. Now if we are children, then we are heirs—heirs of God and co-heirs with Christ, if indeed we share in his sufferings in order that we may also share in his glory. I consider that our present sufferings are not worth comparing with the glory that will be revealed in us.

-Romans 8:16-18

No matter what you've been through, no matter what you're going through right now, no matter what you'll go through one day down the road, it all pales in comparison to the glory that will be revealed in you. What lies ahead outweighs the sufferings of this world by such a margin it's ridiculous. It is literally unfathomable to grasp how much better the Kingdom of God is than all the garbage the world can dish out. So when the world calls you a failure, when a friend turns on you, when a professor antagonizes you, when a family member distances himself from you, when a coach lies to you, when a complete stranger kicks you while you're down--all of it put together doesn't even come close to how amazing your reward is.

Blessed is the man who perseveres under trial, because when he has stood the test, he will receive the crown of life that God has promised to those who love him.

-James 1:12

You can be Lot's wife if you want to[8]. You can look back longingly and wish the world was your friend. Or you can fix your eyes upon Jesus and persevere. You can withstand everything the world throws at you and smile in spite of the pain.

We are so blessed to endure trials. Yeah, I know they suck. And I realize they aren't fun, and I understand how they often don't make sense. But remember that faith must be tested to become more mature. There is no growth without pain. And a crown of life awaits those who persevere under trial.

Jesus conquered the world. We are His legacy. We endure for His sake. He is our reward.

I dare you to pray this:

God, don't remove the difficulties from my life. Instead, grant me a stronger back that I might be able to endure and suffer for You more.

9. Faith

This is the victory that has conquered the world: our faith.

-1 John 5:4

The phrase "conquer the world" usually has a negative connotation. It makes me think of tyrannical dictators and evil super villains. However, according to John, a conqueror is exactly what we should be. We're supposed to possess that world conquering mentality that doesn't give in until we plant our victory flag. But unlike the cliché conquerors, we're not trying to overcome a people or a nation; we're attempting to defeat human nature. We're seeking to overrun the borders of selfishness, hatred, and apathy. And the determining factor is faith.

Our great war is a spiritual war.

Our great depression is our lives.

-Tyler Durden

In Christianity, there is nothing more important than faith. Faith is where everything else stems from; without it, there is no Christianity. Faith is living in a way that makes absolutely no sense unless Jesus really is who He says He is. It takes faith to believe that He is the way, the truth, and the life. It takes faith to love God more than anything else. And it definitely takes faith to love your neighbor as yourself. Faith is believing there's more to this existence than just what we can see. And it's faith that you'll have to cling to when your life falls off the hinges.

Over the next few years, your faith is going to go through hell. Professors, friends, strangers, relatives, coaches and anyone else you can think of are going to put your faith to the test. Some will attack it directly. They'll debate your theology or beliefs, and they'll try to get you to see it their way. Other times, you won't even realize your faith is being tested. But through it all, you have an opportunity to conquer college. You've got a chance to plant a flag on top of the tallest building on campus and to smile while you do it. But it's going to take faith.

Liquid

Too often we allow our faith to be a liquid. It's pretty good if life stays calm. As long as the wind doesn't blow and the ground doesn't shake, there aren't any ripples. But then what happens? People start throwing rocks at it, so it splashes and sloshes around. Then, people come and dip out of it; they bring buckets and scoop out all they can. Then, someone finds a hole, and it just starts pouring out all over the place.

Your faith can't be a liquid if you want it to survive college. If your faith just streams along taking the shape of whatever you pour it in to, it will eventually either dry up or get trapped in a container that's not God. Your faith must be a solid.

Matter is one of the coolest things to learn about. And one thing I've learned is that the particles that make up matter are constantly moving. It's the speed at which they move that determines if the matter is a solid, liquid, or gas. The book you are currently holding is obviously a solid, but on the microscopic level, its particles are flying around. The particles aren't moving fast enough to make it a liquid or a gas, but they're moving all the same. Faith in God works the same way. Your faith is constantly moving. Relationships, circumstances, and life events are continuously shaping your perception and understanding of God. The particles of your faith are flying around everywhere. But it's how fast you allow them to move that determines if your faith is solid or liquid.

In our society, we are big on instant gratification. It seems like nearly everyone has a "what have you done for me lately" attitude. And then we let that same mindset apply to God. We don't see a blessing for a while or can't figure out how a dreadful situation is going to turn out for good, and the particles of our faith start to speed up. Then, we fail to reach a goal or a relationship falls apart, and the particles speed up even more. And after a relatively short amount of time, that faith has become a liquid, and we're just itching to pour it into a new container.

Patience is an incredible virtue, especially when it comes to faith. About a year ago, I got a Facebook message from a lady my mom used to work for. I don't know if this woman was drunk or what was going on, but she proceeded to tell me how terrible a person my mother was. She claimed my mom had stolen her $40,000 dollar wedding ring and other various items and called my mother a liar and a thief. (Did I mention this was through Facebook.) After I read it, I sat back and contemplated for a few minutes. None of it was in my mom's character, and it just didn't seem to add up, so I called my mom. I told her the situation, and I read her the message. And then I laughed. I laughed a good, hard laugh. The message was so preposterous I couldn't do anything but laugh. I asked my mom why she hadn't pawned the ring, paid off all her bills and moved to the beach. Why was she struggling to make rent if she had all those diamonds sitting around her apartment? I still chuckle when I think about that message.

This apparently delusional woman was doing her best to get me to throw my own mother under the bus. She was hoping that message would splinter my relationship with my mom and that I would turn on her. And it very well could have worked. I could have jumped to conclusions and assumed my mother was in fact a liar and a thief. I could have called her up and yelled at her for committing such crimes. But I had patience. I thought about the twenty-three years that I had known my mother. I considered how she treats people on a daily basis. I contemplated the character of the lady who had sent the message. And it wasn't long before I was laughing at how outlandish the thought of my mom stealing a $40,000 dollar ring was. I have this image in my head of my mom sliding down a cable in a room full of security cameras and lasers and swiping the ring mission impossible style. It's ridiculous.

So, if I wouldn't throw my mother under the bus, why would I ever throw God? If I consider his style, timing, and winning percentage, why would I ever think He wasn't going to come through? If I contemplate His character, love, and nature, why would I ever think He had forsaken me? If you really sit back and think about who God is and how God is, it makes absolutely no sense to ever let faith become a liquid. Sure, the particles of your faith are going to move around, but after everything He has done, why would you ever let that faith pour in to something else?

Understanding

It's hard to have a strong faith if you don't actually understand it. It's like trying to explain how to read when you don't know the alphabet. It's probably not going to turn out so well. And I understand how busy college life is, but it's important to take the time to figure out something as monumental as faith. I know you have a lot to study already, but you really need to study the Bible if you want to further your relationship with God. (And don't just read it; do what it says.)

Not too long ago, I heard a preacher equate all the activities of life to a cafeteria tray. As a person moves down the line, he places each activity into a compartment on his tray. And as he continues, he runs out of room, and eventually there's nowhere to put God on the tray. It's a fairly cliché concept, and I'm sure you've heard something similar. However, I don't think it's a very good illustration. I don't see God as just another entrée that needs to be slopped down in an open compartment. I see God as the tray. All our activities should be placed in Him. The thought shouldn't be "I have to fit God in somewhere." It should be "Now, how do I fit this into God?" He should be the foundation. But you can't have a strong foundation without understanding your faith.

Would you build the foundation of a house without understanding how to pour concrete? Would you trust a foundation built by someone who didn't understand erosion, water runoff, or just the basic concepts of underpinning a house? So why would your foundation with God be any different?

I've got a friend whose mother, Shelia, is desperately trying to be cool. She's one of those mothers who tries to keep up with "what the kids are saying nowadays." And she recently got in to texting. Well, of course she wanted to be able to communicate well with her children so she started using all the acronyms and emojis that are prevalent in texting language. The only problem was that she didn't quite know what all those acronyms stood for. Like "lol" for instance. Shelia thought it stood for "lots of love." This made for a very disconcerting message when Shelia's mother had a heart attack, and she sent out the text "Grandma's in the hospital...lol."

It's important to understand your faith. Don't just assume you know what it means; you might end up like Shelia who accidentally laughs at an elderly woman's near death experience. I realize how much you've got going on. Between all the classes, parties, intramurals, naps, and procrastination that you have to do, I can see how it would be hard to fit God into your schedule. But it's not about fitting Him in. Seek Him first; make Him the foundation. Then, let everything else fall into place.

...continue to work out your salvation with fear and trembling

-Philippians 2:12

Think about salvation, faith, and your relationship with God as a gigantic calculus problem. And I mean this thing is huge. It's got tons of sections and letters and it just goes on and on and on.

Now, at first glance, the problem is just daunting. It's way too big to ever think about solving. But you decide to be a Christian, and you start working it out. You take it section by section, and you start figuring out different parts of it. Four years go by, and you get one piece of it solved. Ten years go by, and another section gets figured out. Twenty-five years go by, and some more parts make sense. And so on and so forth until you die and finally figure out what X was actually equal to.

You're never gonna understand everything about your faith until you can actually talk to the Creator face to face. As long as you're on the Earth, you'll have questions that simply can't be answered. But that doesn't mean you don't work your butt off to answer them. And you're more than welcome to let the next few years roll by without trying to understand your faith better. Once again, that's your choice. But trust me when I tell you that there is absolutely no better opportunity to learn about God and what it means to be a Christian than in college. You currently have more energy, resources, and free time to gain a better understanding of faith than you ever will again. So don't let this opportunity slip away.

Test yourselves to see if you are in the faith. Examine yourselves.

-2 Corinthians 13:5

Basically, what Paul and Timothy were saying was "Check yourself before you wreck yourself." If you truly examine your life, are you in the faith? Are you living in a way that seeks God first? Are you studying the Bible? Are you involved with a group of Christians? Are you doing your absolute best to understand your faith?

I'm not talking about religion. I'm not wondering if you earned enough religion points for the week, so now you can feel good about yourself. You held the door open for someone—2 points. You said no to smoking pot—5 points. Oh, you went to church—50 points. It's not about rules, regulations, and religion. Where's your heart? How's your relationship with God? That's what matters.

For we did not follow cleverly contrived myths when we made known to you the power and coming of our Lord Jesus Christ; instead, we were eyewitnesses of His majesty.

-1 Peter 1:16

Are you an eyewitness of His majesty? Could someone come to you and get an eyewitness account of how incredible Jesus is? Or are you so focused on doing your own thing that you don't even see Him pass by?

Without an understanding of what Jesus is like, it is impossible to be an eyewitness of His majesty. And without that understanding, it is impossible to live as He lived. It's not about religion. It's not about playing church. It's not about regurgitating Bible stories or reciting verses. It's about understanding who Jesus is and how incredible a relationship with Him can be.

You have the time. You have the resources. You have the opportunity. There's no excuse for graduating without understanding what it means to have a true relationship with Christ. Your understanding won't be anywhere close to perfect. The calculus problem of faith will be a long way from solved. But the effort you put in now will bring you that much closer to seeing the face of God. There's only one thing in this life that's worth understanding; don't put it off until the end.

Work, Hard Work

Works don't get you in to Heaven. There is no "good enough." We are saved by grace, and that's all there is to it. There's nothing you can do to earn your way in. At the same time, your life should look different than the lives of non-Christians. There should be no question about where you put your faith, and it's through works that the world knows you're a Christian.

What good is it, my brothers, if a man claims to have faith but has no deeds? Can such faith save him? Suppose a brother or sister is without clothes and daily food. If one of you says to him, "Go, I wish you well; keep warm and well fed," but does nothing about his physical needs, what good is it? In the same way, faith by itself, if it is not accompanied by action, is dead.

-James 2:14-17

It's impossible to be a living, breathing Christian and not do good deeds. The two go hand in hand. Without deeds, faith is dead. If faith is dead, there's no relationship with Christ. It's that simple. There's no such thing as a faith without deeds.

One common problem people have with grace is that it suggests that a person can sin all he wants, and no matter what, God will forgive him. They see grace as a free pass to live an evil life, and then at the end, cash in a get out of hell free card. But if the Holy Spirit is truly in a person, is it even possible for him to live an evil life? I don't think so. If someone is completely honest and serious when he makes Jesus the sovereign of his life, it's impossible for him to purposefully live in sin and consistently commit wrongful actions. Now, everyone falls short of perfection. There's no doubt about that at all. Every Christian screws up; every Christian makes terrible mistakes and poor decisions. However, the thought that a person could be a Christian and at the same time knowingly live a wretched, sinful life waiting to cash in on grace at the end is preposterous. You either love God or you love the sin. A person can't serve both.

In the same way, a Christian cannot possibly have faith in God and not have good works to go along with it. The problem is we talk about faith and works like their separate entities, but they're not. Good works aren't something that happen independently and get tacked on to faith; they're a part of faith. Faith and works are two sides of the same coin.

This is another reason why it's hard work being a Christian. Not because work gets you in, but because once you're in, you can't help but work your butt off. Once you receive God's spirit, the work just comes with the territory. And it's tough. It's hard to be nice to the girl in class who won't stop asking stupid questions. It's hard to forgive the friend who is now dating your ex. It's hard to tithe ten percent of your paycheck when you're struggling to make rent. It's hard to pray for the roommate who has sex in the bed next to you. It's hard to reach out to the guy who is constantly putting you down. It's hard work. But it's what you signed up for. The work is just part of being a Christian. Once again, they aren't separate entities. They go hand in hand.

The work is simply something expected from us. Your parents expect certain things from you. Maybe it's to mow the lawn or take out the garbage. Perhaps it's to keep your room clean and do all your homework. Now that you're in college, they probably expect you to call home every now and then to keep them updated on your life. And I'm sure they expect you to graduate. (Especially if they're paying for it.) Now, meeting those expectations doesn't make you their child. Whether you take the trash out or not won't change your DNA. Instead, it's because you're their child that they expect those things out of you. It works the same way with God. Good deeds won't make you His child. It's because you're His child that you're expected to do good deeds.

The only thing that counts is faith expressing itself through love.

-Galatians 5:6

I love this verse's simplicity. Unlike a lot of other verses in the Bible, this one is black and white. It says the *only* thing—not one of the main things or one of the numerous things—but the *only* thing that counts is faith working through love. Can a person be a Christian and not love? Of course not. The greatest commandments are love God and love people. But why is that? It's because love expresses your faith. You can't love a God who you don't have faith in. You can't love your enemy, or even your neighbor for that matter, without having faith that Jesus was right when He said it was how to live. Love is faith in action.

It's amazing how hard it is to love people. On a daily basis we come into contact with people we don't know, but how often do we share Christ with them? We all have friends who aren't Christians, but how often do we invite those people to church? How often do we truly show the kind of love that God expects from us? Here's the real question: How much do you have to hate someone to not tell him about Jesus?

If you honestly believe that He is the way, the truth, and the life—If you really know that Christianity is the best possible way to live—then how on earth can you let someone pass through your life without sharing Christ with them? If you see a man starving to death, do you just say "good luck" and pass on by? No, you give him something to eat. So why is it different when we meet someone starving for Jesus?

Now, I'm not trying to make you feel guilty. Every Christian I know struggles with this, and it's quite possibly the hardest part of being a Christian. But again, it's just part of it. Christianity is hard work. Don't let anyone tell you different.

And without faith it is impossible to please God, because anyone who comes to Him must believe that He exists and that He rewards those who earnestly seek Him.

-Hebrews 11:6

Are you earnestly seeking God right now? For a while, I thought I was, but it was really all just pretend. I was good at the outside stuff. I didn't have too much trouble loving people. But on the inside, I was wretched. My actions and deeds showed I was a Christian, but my heart wasn't earnestly seeking Jesus. In other words, my faith was operating at fifty percent. And fifty percent just doesn't cut it. I mean, a fifty gets you an F. To put it bluntly, my relationship with God sucked. And it sucked because I wasn't putting effort into it.

Because we serve a supernatural God, Christians often think their relationships with Him will also happen supernaturally. I figured my relationship with Him was good because I was helping others and doing good works, but that wasn't the case at all. A relationship with God works very similarly to any other relationship. It requires time, work, and understanding through communication. And just like anything else you want to be good at, it requires practice.

Think about when you were first learning how to drive. More than likely, you weren't very good when you initially started out. If an emergency had required you to rush someone to the hospital, it probably wouldn't have turned out so well. But after a few years of driving, as you practiced more and more, you probably became fairly proficient at it. If an emergency required you to make haste to the hospital today, it wouldn't be nearly as difficult. A relationship with God works the same way. The more time and energy you put in to it, the better it gets. It's not magic. There's no secret formula. The more you practice, the stronger it becomes.

That's why reading the Bible is so important. That's why spending time in prayer is such a big deal. That's why studying and learning more about Him matters so much. If you fell in love with someone, would you just hang out with him every now and then? Would you only talk to her when life was really crappy? Would you only learn more about him when you had nothing else to do? Would you only listen to her when your life was falling apart?

So, if you truly love God, why would you treat your relationship with Him any differently than a relationship with any other person you love? Does a person on this earth deserve more of your faith than God?

This whole Christianity thing takes a lot of work. Hard work. And honestly, most people aren't up to it. (The gate is small and the way is narrow after all.) But I promise the work never goes unrewarded. So be honest: Is your faith alive and well? Or deedless and dead? Does your faith express itself through love? Or does your faith lack action? Are you earnestly seeking God both inside and out? Or are you neglecting an important aspect of your faith?

When something is easy, the end result is rarely very exciting. So considering how difficult Christianity is, what does that tell you about the final outcome?

The Grind

I realize how tough it is to be a Christian day in and day out. We all grow weary at one point or another. We all get a little burnt out from time to time. Maybe it's hard to see where God's leading you, or you've hit a spiritual wall. Maybe you feel stuck in divine limbo, or the answer to a question is taking its sweet time. Whatever the case may be, reflection and perseverance will get you through. You just have to keep showing up—keep grinding— and let God bring your faith to completion.

Reflection is key when you feel your spiritual life falling into a rut. Where is your joy? Not your happiness, it's fickle. Happiness changes all the time. But joy is a constant; it's not easily swayed. Where's yours? Have you been putting it into the world that is temporary? Or do you truly find joy in God? How often do you reflect on all the ways God has worked and is working in your life? It's important. It doesn't take long before we're quick to forget God and even quicker to blame Him. Stopping to think and dwell on how awesome He is and how much He loves you can make your situation less daunting. God realizes it's a grind. It's not like He doesn't see you there. And I'm pretty sure He was clear on the road being tough. Don't get so caught in the rut that you lose track of what you're after.

When you start to feel a little burnt out, make sure it's not because you've become selfish. Are you seeking bigger and better mission trips to really spread Jesus or because the smaller ones you used to go on don't give you the same rush anymore? Are you looking for new ways to serve because it's what God's leading you to do or because you want more glory? Are you hopping from one worship service to the next because you truly want to find the best fit or because you only like singing certain songs and hearing certain messages? Have you made the relationship about you? Are you chasing the work instead of God?

Once again, you need to reflect on your motives and be honest about your relationship. Dwell on all the reasons you put faith in Him in the first place, and make sure you're really seeking *His* glory, *His* fame, and what's best for *His* kingdom. You can bullcrap yourself, but you can't bullcrap God.

[D]o not grow weary of doing good.

-2 Thessalonians 3:13

After reflection, when you've really come to terms with your relationship, it's possible that you're living unselfishly and actively seeking His glory; yet, everyday still feels like a grind. My best advice? Get over it. Anyone who has ever been great at something had to push through the grind and persevere when everything in and around them said to quit. Whether it was mastering an instrument, playing a sport, or deciphering complex equations, they had to press on toward their goals. Greatness is expensive, especially in matters of faith. No matter how insignificant it may seem, never get tired of doing good. Pursue God an inch at the time if you have to.

[W]e must not get tired of doing good, for we will reap at the proper time if we don't give up.

-Galatians 6:9

The grind is another way to sharpen your faith. It's just another test. It's one more way for your faith to become mature. The key is never giving up. I know it gets tough sometimes, and it feels like life has torn your faith to pieces, but you must not give in. The proper time is coming. Sorrow may last for the night, but joy comes with the morning. Is your faith strong enough to hold on until daybreak? Do you have it in you to keep grinding it out? Can you force yourself to not grow weary and trust that God knows what He's doing? Are you able to just let go and let God and have faith in His timing?

Remember this: Whoever sows sparingly will also reap sparingly, and whoever sows generously will also reap generously.

-2 Corinthians 9:6

This isn't complex math. There's no secret formula. It says it right there in Second Corinthians: sow small, reap small; sow big, reap big. This especially applies when faith becomes a grind. It's easy to trust God when everything's easy. Putting faith in Him works out really well when the road is smooth. We don't have much problem sowing generously when life is under control. But how much do you sow when it all comes tumbling down? What about when it feels like faith has failed you? Then, it seems like a much larger risk to sow wholeheartedly. I mean, you could fail and life could get even worse. And it's easy to get scared of the fact that if you sow more, you have more to lose.

But here's the deal: if you want to reap great things, you have to sow greatly. Some people have the mindset of "never try, never fail," and I'm sure they live very safe, uncomplicated lives. But what does that kind of life look like to God? Is the Bible full of stories about people who were afraid to risk anything? Not even close. It gives account after account of people who risked absolutely everything for their faith and stuck it out no matter what. How much of a grind do you think it was for Paul spending all that time in prison? Yet, he never lost the faith. In his deepest, darkest moments, his faith shined through and brought people to Christ. Yes, if you risk more, you stand to lose more. There's no doubt about that. **But risking nothing costs you everything**. So, push through the grind by putting full faith in God. After all, it is the victory that conquered the world.

Nothing in this world can take the place of PERSISTENCE. Talent will not; nothing is more common than unsuccessful people with talent. Genius will not; unrewarded genius is almost a proverb. Education will not; the world is full of educated derelicts. PERSISTENCE and DETERMINATION alone are omnipotent. The slogan "PRESS ON" has solved and always will solve the problems of the human race.

-Calvin Coolidge

10. One Pass

I expect to pass though this world but once; any good
therefore that I can do, or any kindness that I can show to
any fellow creature, let me do it now; let me not defer or
neglect it, for I shall not pass this way again.

-Stephen Grellet

I love Stephen Grellet's quote because of the ending. "I shall
not pass this way again." One pass, one go round, one
opportunity. That's it. Before you know it you're standing before
the judge in heaven and answering for your life's work. And
that's not just a metaphor, that's Bible.

For we must all appear before the judgment seat of Christ, that
each one may receive what is due to him for the things done while
in the body, whether good or bad.

-2 Corinthians 5:10

We'll all stand before the judge. My question is if you died
today and stood before Him, would you be proud of your work?
A lot of Christians do their absolute best to live as safe and
comfortable as possible. But I look through the Bible, and I read its
stories, and I just don't see that whole safe and comfortable thing
at all. In Hebrews eleven, Paul writes about some of the great
people of God.

Some men were tortured, not accepting release, so that they might gain a better resurrection, and others experienced mocking and scourging, as well as bonds and imprisonment. They were stoned, they were sawed in two, they died by the sword, they wandered about in sheepskins, in goat skins, destitute, afflicted and mistreated.

The world was not worthy of them.

-Hebrews 11:35-38

You might read that and think, well, those are the all time greats Paul is writing about. They were the Bible all-stars. They were special. They're way above anything I could ever be.

Really?

Because if you turn over to James five, it says:

Elijah was a man just like us.

-James 5:17

Do you remember Elijah? Do you remember what happened in First Kings? I'll paraphrase.

There were 450 prophets of the god Baal shouting up at the sky. All day long they called out for Baal to answer them. And they're cutting themselves and dancing around their altar just trying to get some sort of a sign. Then Elijah, a single prophet, comes and builds an altar. And he makes a sacrifice to God, the real God, and says "Answer me, O Lord, answer me, so these people will know that you, O Lord, are God, and that you are turning their hearts back again."

And fire falls down from heaven.

When everyone sees it they fall to the ground crying out, "The Lord—he is God! The Lord—he is God!"

In James, it says the man who called fire down from heaven was no more special than any one of us. He was merely a man. Nothing more. Nothing less.

So what's holding you back? Is it fear? Are you scared to get out of your comfort zone?

God has not given us a spirit of fearfulness, but one of power, love, and sound judgment.

-2 Timothy 1:7

God didn't create you to be afraid. He hasn't given you a spirit of fearfulness.

Therefore, we may boldly say:
     The Lord is my helper;
     I will not be afraid.
     What can man do to me?

-Hebrews 13:6

No fear. Walk boldly.

Here's the deal: there aren't going to be any cowards in heaven. I look through the Bible and I just don't see cowards. I see a lot of regular people who put faith in God and did some incredible things. I'm not saying they weren't ever afraid, but their faith far outweighed their fear.

Then again, maybe it's not fear that holds you back. Maybe it's time. Maybe you've filled up your life with so much stuff that spreading the gospel just isn't convenient. Maybe all the classes, intramurals, parties, and naps are getting in the way.

[P]roclaim the message; persist in it whether convenient or not

-2 Timothy 4:2

Is God getting in the way of your life? Or is your life getting in the way of God? We often want everything to be just right. We want the lighting to be good. We want the music to sound a certain way. We want the mood to be perfect. We do everything we can to love and serve people on our own terms and in our own time. But just for the record, that's not even close to Biblical. Christianity isn't about what's convenient for you. And it's definitely not about fitting God into *your* busy schedule.

One of the great uses of Twitter and Facebook will be to prove at the Last Day that prayerlessness was not from lack of time.

-John Piper

But maybe it's not fear, and it's not time that you're hung up on. Maybe it's your age. You might still be a teenager for all I know. And you might be having a hard time believing a college kid can really make an impact. I mean, what can young people do to change the world anyway, right?

And let's be honest, the world doesn't really expect much out of us. We're young, and we're Christians. Yeah, the world doesn't think we're capable of anything really. The churches we grew up in probably don't even believe we'll account for much—at least not until we're older. Think about it. When we hear stories about how people used to get married at sixteen and have kids, we're appalled. Not because it's wrong but because we don't think we could handle that kind of responsibility. We're sad that they didn't get to have as much fun as we're having. But what happened? Did people all of a sudden change? Did our generation's genes get altered? No. Society just started expecting less and less from us, and for some reason we obliged. Our culture set the bar low, and we were happy to barely climb over it. We've accepted the status quo of the world. We've accepted the status quo of the church. And that doesn't sit well with me.

Most parents today would tell you that "kids grow up too fast." If you don't believe that, just go find a ten year old and ask to borrow her cell phone. But for some reason, around the age of eighteen, that growing up comes to a complete halt. Now, I'm all about having a youthful spirit and a child like faith, but when it comes to taking on responsibilities, making tough choices, and loving God, you have got to grow up. Don't just keep pushing adolescence back. That's how you end up as a twenty-three year old senior who has no clue what to do with his life and has to move back in with mom after graduation and get babied for a couple more years. Don't be that guy.

Young people have incredible power to change things. Why? Because they haven't bought the lies of this world yet. They still believe in hope. They still have the guts to lay it all on the line to create a better tomorrow. I mean, the disciples were teenagers when Jesus first called them. Why would the Son of God handpick that group of young men if they weren't able to completely revolutionize the entire planet? Apparently, young people have it in them. But do you live like it?

Don't let anyone look down on you because you are young, but set an example for the believers in speech, in life, in love, in faith, and in purity.

-1 Timothy 4:12

I'm sure you've been hearing that verse since you were coloring outside the lines in Sunday school, but be honest, are you living down to the expectations that society and the church have for you? Or are you an example for what a true Christ-follower should look like?

Then again, you might realize young people can change the world, but you're looking at all this God stuff and thinking you're way too young to devote your life to it. Now's the time to party anyway, right? Isn't college when you live it up and feel bad about it later?

Flee the evil desires of youth, and pursue righteousness, faith, love and peace, along with those who call on the Lord out of a pure heart.

-2 Timothy 2:22

I'm not saying you should lock yourself away in your dorm room, surround yourself with Bibles, and sing hymns all day. The question is what are you pursuing? Are you pursuing the parties? Or are you going to parties to get to know people and make sure they don't drive away drunk? Are you pursuing the intramurals? Or are you pursuing opportunities to tell the people on your intramural team about Jesus? I've learned that it's less about what you're doing and more about who you're seeking. It's about finding a way to do everything for the glory of God.

A few guys in the youth group at my church really took that idea to heart. I think it might have started out as a smart alec type thing, but they said, "Well, if we should do everything for the glory of God, I guess we should start playing XBOX for His glory." So they started having mini Bible studies while playing Halo. They're blowing each other up and talking about Jesus. And they're all at different houses talking on headsets over the internet. After a couple times, a friend of theirs who wasn't a

Christian started playing with them and listening in on the conversations. Then he started asking questions. Then he wanted to know Jesus.

I want you to know that that kid gave his life to Christ while playing XBOX. He said the sinner's prayer and started following Jesus because a group of Christians decided to play video games for the glory of God.

See, I don't play sports just because they make me happy. I play sports so I can meet people and tell them about Jesus. You don't go to class just so you can earn a degree. You don't go to work just so you can make money. You do those things so you can meet people and tell them about Jesus.

How much do you have to hate someone to not tell them about Jesus?

It's like standing on the sidewalk and seeing someone about to get hit by a bus and not yelling for them to get out of the way. I mean, how much do you have to hate someone to just stand by and watch them get hit by a bus?

What if we stopped standing idly by? What if we stopped making excuses?

I had an incredible strength coach when I played football in college. I remember one time during summer workouts when a bunch of guys on the team were complaining about how hard the workouts were and how sore their legs were. And they were making all sorts of excuses as to why they weren't doing well.

After one workout, the strength coach gathered us up around him and he said, "Men, I know a lot of you are having a rough time. I realize a lot of you are dealing with some pretty serious soreness. And I want you to know that there are three things you can do for soreness: **Eat. Hydrate. And get over it.**"

As Christians, we often need to follow the same advice. When it's hard to live out the Bible, when it's easy to just make excuses, and when it's tough to love God and love people, we need to eat, hydrate, and get over it.

Response

So, now what? After all this, what's your response going to be? I remember a couple years ago when I volunteered to lead a group of middle schoolers at a big youth weekend. I was telling them about Jesus and explaining to them what it meant to be a Christian and what that kind of life looks like. Then I remember getting home from the weekend and realizing how different my life was from the one I told those young students to lead. I realized my response to Jesus was a joke.

I knew all about Jesus. I knew what I was supposed to be doing. I knew where my time and energy were supposed to be going. I knew what my relationship with Jesus was supposed to be like. But I wasn't living up to the gospel. I was making excuses. I was building my own kingdom. I was pursuing myself. To put it plainly, my life didn't make any sense.

Because based on what I knew about God, based on His love for me, based on Jesus' sacrifice on my behalf, the only thing that made sense was to completely devote my life to Him. If I truly believed that the greatest commandments were to love God and love people, then the only thing that could possibly make sense was to give everything I had to love God and love people. If I truly believed that hell was a real place and anyone who didn't know Jesus was going to spend eternity there, then the only thing that could possibly make sense was to tell people about Jesus.

I'm not asking you to live radically. I'm not asking you to go out on a limb and do something crazy. I'm asking you to live the only life that makes sense. And what makes sense is handing your life completely over to God. What makes sense is loving Him and loving others with all that is in you. What makes sense is passionately pursuing Him on a daily basis.

Knowing what you know, not giving God everything is

what's radical. That's what's crazy.

And I just want you to realize that you have the power to do some incredibly amazing things. One of my absolute favorite verses is in John fourteen where Jesus says:

I tell you the truth, anyone who has faith in me will do what I have been doing. And he will do even greater things than these, because I am going to the Father.

-John 14:12

Jesus says it Himself. You have the power to do even greater things than He did. Do you believe that?

Christianity is not about just getting by. It's not about finding a way to sneak in the back door of heaven. Not at all. You've heard the phrase 24/7/365. Well, Christianity is about 25/8/366 and 367 on leap year. It's all day, every day. It's about going to the grave with nothing left to give. Jesus has challenged us to live in such a way that we can stand before God with sweat dripping down our faces and with calluses on our hands, that we might look the Creator of the universe in the eye and say, "I used everything you gave me. Every ounce of talent. Every shred of ability. Every drop of energy. And it was all for your glory so that people on earth would know what heaven looks like and give you praise."

That's Christianity.

So what is your response? What is your reaction? You only get one pass; what are you going to do with it?

Afterword

Jesus replied, "No one who puts his hand to the plow and looks back is fit for service in the kingdom of God."

-Luke 9:62

Let's just be honest here. Being a Christian in college comes with a high cost. Christianity pretty much goes against the entire collegiate way of life, and it requires you to look at the world in a way that is completely different from your non-Christian classmates. Maintaining a Christian lifestyle will require all the energy, strength, and self-discipline you have. Not that you won't slip up—you're going to fail over and over again, I assure you. But I don't say this to deter you; I just want you to know what you're getting into.

Christianity isn't for people who look back. Luke 9:62 is very clear on that. When preparing a field to plant crops, it was imperative that the person guiding the plow kept his eyes forward. If he ever looked back, the oxen pulling the plow would move off the line and make the row crooked. And if one row was crooked, each row following it would be even more crooked.

In the same way, you can't take on the life of a Christian while still loving the world and regretting everything you had to give up. You can't go into this half-heartedly. You have to be all in.

In other words, don't put your hand to the plow without weighing the cost.

"Suppose one of you wants to build a tower. Will he not first sit down and estimate the cost to see if he has enough money to complete it? For if he lays the foundation and is not able to finish it, everyone who sees it will ridicule him, saying, 'This fellow began to build and was not able to finish.'

 Or suppose a king is about to go to war against another king. Will he not first sit down and consider whether he is able with ten thousand men to oppose the one coming against him with twenty thousand? If he is not able, he will send a delegation while the other is still a long way off and will ask for terms of peace. In the same way, any of you who does not give up everything he has cannot be my disciple."

-Luke 14:28-33

I've said it before, and I'll say it again: Christianity is the toughest thing you will ever do. It requires sacrifice after sacrifice. It requires letting go of the comforts and pleasures of this world. Count the cost before you tread down this path. Jesus never said it would be easy. But He said He would always be there.

And surely I am with you always, to the very end of the age.

-Matthew 28:20

So I guess the question is: Do you have what it takes?

Do you have what it takes to actually follow Jesus in college? Frankly, a lot of people don't. The road is difficult, and the gate to the kingdom is narrow after all. And it's been said that few find it. Do you have it in you to be one of the few?

I hope so.

I hope you don't make excuses. I hope you realize blaming your parents for your lot in life has an expiration date. I hope you understand how much Jesus sacrificed on your behalf. I hope you take on the life He is calling you to. I hope you weigh the cost, put your hand to the plow, and never look back.

Notes

1. There's absolutely nothing wrong with being an investment banker; it's simply completely opposite of *my* talents and passion.

2. 1 Peter 5:7

3. Mark 12:30-31

4. Fun fact, from freshman year to senior year, I gained forty-three pounds. Thanks football.

5. A quote from Vince Lombardi. If you don't know much about him, I highly suggest you look him up.

6. According to dictionary.com, debauchery is excessive indulgence in sensual pleasures; intemperance.

7. I spent a large part of my college career as a designated driver. But I had a few rules:

- I never drove my own car. That way I wasn't using up my own gas, and if someone threw up in the floor board, it wasn't my problem. For the record, I drove the car of whoever I was designated driving for. I didn't borrow some random friend's car to cart around drunk people. That would be messed up.

- If the people in the car wanted me to take them to get some food, someone had to buy me a meal of equal or lesser value to their own. That's a pretty fair payment.

- No open containers in the car. That's a good way to get arrested.

8. Genesis 19:26

About the Author

Gabe Barrett grew up in Alexander City, Alabama before moving to Kentucky to finish out high school. He attended three universities during his five year college career. Gabe served as an RA, worked in the IT department, acted as president of a residential college, and even played football for Auburn University during that time. He graduated with a degree in English and is currently working on a number of books. He conquered college in 2010.

Gabe is also the director of the M25 Mission Camp in Atlanta, Georgia where he organizes and leads mission trips for high school and college students to work with the homeless.

Made in the USA
Columbia, SC
14 May 2021

37370944R10098